In Praise of *Writing and Experiential Educat...*

"*Writing and Experiential Education* offers instructors the unique opportunity to explore the relationship between concrete experiences and abstract writing practices. It highlights the importance of differentiating the presentation and explanation of subject matter not only to meet the needs of students, but also to grow their confidence as writers."

Molly Cummings, Ed.M., English Teacher, Boston, MA

"A must-have, go-to guide for any teacher who is looking to improve writing education. 21st Century classroom instruction for adolescents demands creativity, flexibility, and authenticity. Rapparlie makes experientialism's link to writing clear in these detailed step-by-step lesson plans for thinking and learning—adding depth to any progressive educator's repertoire."

Amelia Menut Duffy, English Teacher and Literacy Specialist

"Rapparlie's approach highlights the experiential nature of learning to write and gives teachers ideas they can use in their own classrooms for engaging students with the writing process. The experiential paradigm that informs all of her activities becomes a powerful model for designing original classroom activities that fit your topic. In this way Rapparlie not only gives you some nice lures to help hook your students on the writing process, she also teaches you to fish so you can design a curriculum specifically angled to the stream of knowledge that flows through your class."

Michael Goeller, Associate Director, Rutgers University-New Brunswick Writing Program

"Here is a demonstration of writing's natural connection to experiential learning. The ready-to-go activities and lessons are thoughtful, creative and time-savers for educators. The activities and rationale support writing across the curriculum and character/values education, which is a focus of many educators in the 21st century. The activities are clearly explained, well organized, and include useful debriefing suggestions—ideal for novice to more advanced practitioners."

Jen Lara, Professor of Education and Blogger

"Leslie Rapparlie's book fills an important gap in the literature on experiential learning. It is a creative piece of work that discusses important writing techniques. Useful and practical information for educators—I highly recommend it to anyone interested in engaging their students in the writing process."

Scott D. Wurdinger, Professor of Experiential Education and Leadership Studies, Minnesota State University, Mankato

"This book has exceptional potential for classroom teachers! The framework and theory provided are written clearly. The examples are helpful. I love the lesson plans! There are multiple uses for classroom teachers and content area teachers in science and social studies. I would encourage all of my schools to study, implement, and reflect on the lessons and activities outlined in this book!"

Jennifer Seydel, Ph.D., School Designer, Midwest Region, Expeditionary Learning Schools, Madison, WI

"Rapparlie captures her vast experience working with people in engaging ways with her love for the craft of writing, assisting educators of many disciplines to reach audiences with a renewed spark. Her selection of activities within the text will captivate students to think critically, perform socially and reflect internally. This subject is a text that is in-demand, giving educators new tools to teach critical content following methodology that is effective."

Sam Steiger, Director, Adventure Education Program, Minnesota State University, Mankato

WRITING
AND EXPERIENTIAL
EDUCATION

PRACTICAL ACTIVITIES AND LESSON
PLANS TO ENRICH LEARNING

Leslie Rapparlie

WOODNBARNES
open books • open minds

Published by:

WOODNBARNES Publishing
2309 N. Willow, Bethany, OK 73008
(405) 942-6812

Figure 1.1: Adapted, with permission, from Evans, Forney and Guido-Dibrito

Figure 1.2: Adapted, with permission, from L. Rapparlie, 2009, How do we learn? An exploration of John Dewey's pattern of inquiry. In *Teaching adventure education theory: Best practices*, edited by B. Stremba and C.A. Bisson (Champaign, IL: Human Kinetics), 129.

Figure 1.3: Excerpt p. 9 from WRITING ACROSS THE CURRICULUM, 3rd ed. by Art Young. Copyrght © 1999 by Prentice-Hall, Inc. Reprinted by permission of Pearson Education, Inc.

Figure 2.3 & 2.4: Reprinted with permission from *That Workshop Book: New Systems and Structure for Classrooms that Read, Think and Write* by Samantha Bennett. Copyright © 2007 by Samantha Bennett. Published by Heinemann, Portsmouth, NH. All rights reserved.

Author Photo on cover by Christine Merson

Interior photos (unless otherwise noted) by Leslie Rapparlie and Jennifer Stanchfield

Cover Design by Blue Designs, azurebrp@yahoo.com
Interior Design by Ramona Cunningham

Printed in the United States of America
Oklahoma City, Oklahoma
ISBN # 978-1-885473-70-7

11 12 13 14 15   10 9 8 7 6 5 4 3 2 1

Acknowledgements

Books are never a product of a single individual. While one person does the writing, the entirety of the knowledge complied in a text is the result of one person's interactions with dozens, if not hundreds, of other people. This book is no exception. All the classes I have taken, the conversations and debates I have participated in, the critical eyes that have reviewed these words before publication are all important components that helped bring this book to fruition. Thank you to everyone who participated, supported, and challenged me along the way.

It almost goes without saying, although it never should, that I am grateful to WOODNBARNES Publishing and all the staff who helped critique and provide feedback along the way, especially Mony Cunningham and Jen Stanchfield for all their time and energy to make this book the best it could be.

Moreover, I would like to thank Dr. Jim Hauser of William Paterson University who helped build my knowledge about writing and how to integrate it across the curriculum. Thank you for your workshops, your mentorship and your willingness to lend a hand when I needed it. Importantly, thank you for your endless commitment to spreading awareness about how to use writing in every discipline.

Also, thank you to Dr. Julie Carlson, Dr. Jasper Hunt, and Dr. Scott Wurdinger of the Experiential Education Department at Minnesota State University, Mankato. Your wealth of knowledge and commitment to your students and peers is why I am able to even begin to write this book.

I am forever indebted to Sam Steiger of the Adventure Education Program at Minnesota State University, Mankato. Your constant support and generous friendship keep me going and your commitment and innovation as an experiential educator have helped shape some of the best parts of this text. Much of the genius here is due to major collaboration with you—for that and so much more, I am grateful.

To another genius in his own right, I must thank Paul "Hutch" Hutchinson of the Boston University Outdoor Education Program who is one of the most creative thinkers I know and a true pioneer in the experiential education field. You bring joy to everyone you are around and truly embody everything good about education and friendship. You also keep Shackelton's memory alive. Thank you for sharing his journey with me.

Thank you also to Darcy Turner, Greg Henderson, the GRAB staff of Gettysburg College (new and old), and Heidi Scheusner and the New Horizons staff of 2004-2005 from Lynchburg College for sharing in my journey, learning with me, and allowing me to learn from you. And, perhaps most importantly, my dear friend, mentor, and source of support, John Regentin. Without you, this book would not exist and my life would not be as full of rich experiences.

I am also grateful to Dr. Emily Renauld, Dr. Michel Goeller and Dr. Bill Magrino of Rutgers University-New Brunswick and Dr. Shanyn Fiske of Rutgers University-Camden for all they have taught me about the field of composition over the years.

Forever and always, thank you to Mom, Dad, Tom, Chris and Ashley for endless support and encouragement. Finally, to all my beloved friends, near and far, for everything that you give me, every day.

Contents

Figures

Lesson Reference Guide

LESSONS	Introductory	Essay/Paper Writing	Reading Skills	Writing Process	Research Writing	Creative Writing/Writer's Workshops
1. Building a Respectful Classroom...	✓					
2. Developing Group Behavior Code	✓					
3. Using Senses—Identifying Learning Styles	✓					
4. Junkyard: Communication, Teamwork or Trust	✓					
5. Experiential Double-Entry Journals	✓	✓	✓	✓	✓	✓
6. The Importance of Writing	✓			✓		
7. Using Observation...	✓	✓	✓			
8. Developing Principles to Support the Writing Process	✓			✓		
9. How to Organize an Essay		✓		✓		
10. Working on Clarity		✓				✓
11. Word Choice		✓				✓
12. Writing a Thesis, Lesson One		✓			✓	
13. Writing a Thesis, Lesson Two		✓			✓	
14. Paragraphs and Topic Sentences		✓			✓	
15. Using Transitions		✓			✓	
16. Conclusions		✓			✓	
17. Learning to Write a Research Paper				✓	✓	
18. Referencing and Works Cited		✓			✓	
19. Critiquing and Feedback		✓	✓	✓	✓	✓
20. Developing a Story or Character						✓
21. Working With Language (for Poetry)						✓
22. Choosing Story and Integrating Research						✓
23. Crafting for Lede (for Journalism)						✓
24. Finding Voice		✓			✓	✓

Introduction

While many texts and articles have examined experiential education and its connections with other fields, such as service-learning or outdoor education, few texts examine its links—as a wide-reaching field—to writing. The integration of the two in any educational setting can prove beneficial to all learners. Yet, there seems to be a need to explore and discuss how writing and experiential education can merge—which is why this book was written. While experiential approaches to education are often rapt with hands-on, active activities to spur thought, writing is taught in a very traditional manner. Of course, in order to write, a student must actually perform the act of writing (which is experiential), but experiential learning can play a larger and more influential role in the field of writing. Instead of simply telling students how to craft a sentence, a concrete activity can be used to show them how to do this, making learning dynamic instead of static. According to many educational theorists, like John Dewey, this type of learning resonates better and creates conduits for further growth in students than lecture alone (Dewey 36-48). It seems that modern students perform best with educational experiences that share information in a variety of ways: orally, visually, and interactively (Wurdinger, *Using Experiential Learning in the Classroom*, 50). Very few students are excited about (or retain information from) a lecture-only course. Since writing is an essential skill to every student's success in school and in future employment, instructors must meet this need. Thus, integrating experiential education techniques into the classroom can deepen a student's learning as well as reach a variety of students with differing educational needs.

While writing brings a tenant of experiential education, namely reflection, into any learning experience, there is a greater role for writing as a tool to help students not only reflect on their experiences, but also to process and understand their thoughts and to discover the value of communication in written form. As a skill essential to success in the future, writing is a proficiency that every individual needs. Thus, it is paramount that educators understand how to integrate writing, more fully, into every learning experience.

It is because writing and experiential education are inextricably connected that this text was written. The book briefly explores where both experiential education and writing are before it examines where they can unite. Very brief histories and foundations of each field are conveyed as well as how each is currently employed in the other. From there, the text makes suggestions about how to expand the use of experiential education in writing and vice a versa. Instructors can find useful and practical information and activities to employ in their classrooms. While many of the activities in this book were designed with adults and college students in mind, with some simple adaptation for specific age groups or other needs, almost all of these activities could work for diverse groups of students.

Perhaps the most useful components of this book are the tried and true lesson plans that provide step-by-step instruction—including materials needed, time required, suggested class size, and suggestions for discussion—on how to teach specific ideas using both writing and experiential education. Lesson plans from one chapter can be altered and used in another. For example, Lessons 1 and 8 use the Shackleton story with activities to experientially teach writing. However, instructors can change them into ways to incorporate writing in alternative settings. One example of this would be for a rope course facility to use the Shackleton lesson plans to teach leadership or other themes and incorporate the writing exercises outlined in the lesson or incorporate exercises from other lessons—like free writing or double-entry journals—to supplement the activities described in that lesson. These kinds of adaptations apply to all of the writing techniques and prompts provided. The overarching idea is that the concepts in this text are versatile and interchangeable. If the format of a lesson plan, as written here, does not match with specific classroom or curriculum needs, change it so it does. While all the possibilities of alterations are not listed in this text, instructors should feel encouraged to use the lessons as foundations and build on them in helpful (and relevant) ways for specific student groups and course material.

Furthermore, since many of the terms in this text are often used interchangeably in regular conversation, it seems important to define them here in the introduction as a point of reference for the rest of the text. These definitions, unless otherwise stated within the subsequent pages, are the ones that this text follows:

- Experiential Education—a process where learning is gained through direct, active—although not necessarily physical—experience. Educational experiences are purposefully chosen to create meaningful, long-lasting learning. Generally, experiential education involves following the experiential learning cycle and is collaborative (Bynum Pickle 14; Dewey 25-50; Stanchfield 5-6; Wurdinger, *Using Experiential Learning in the Classroom*, 7-8).

- Outdoor Education—a process of learning by participating in activities that occur in the outdoors and which do not necessarily need to be high-risk or stressful (Bynum Pickle 13-14; Priest 111).

- Adventure Education—education that often involves high-risk or stressful activities to cultivate learning as well as a change on interpersonal and intra-personal levels. Adventure education is regularly equated to outdoor education but outdoor education is not the only form of adventure education

(Bynum Pickle 13; Priest 111-112). "Adventure includes challenge, moments when participants are on the brink of both success and failure, and finding that both are equally instructive. Adventure is about taking risks, not actual physical risk, but emotional and apparent risk where participants see the natural consequences before them" (Project Adventure).

- Environmental Education—learning by participating in, often, outdoor activities designed to assist a person in developing an environmental consciousness or awareness. The focus is often put on biological concepts as well as how people interact with the environment and how the environment acts and reacts to people (Bynum Pickle 14; Priest 111).

- Service Learning—learning by participating in service activities directly linked to course curriculum that are designed to assist a person in developing a social awareness as well as an understanding of his or her desired role as an informed and engaged citizen. Generally, service learning is not episodic but occurs more frequently and works toward a tangible end product. Students, faculty and staff are all viewed as important partners and contributors to the service project and learning outcomes ("What is Service Learning?").

Since this book focuses on writing and experiential education, it assumes that most readers choose this book to gain new ideas about how to employ experiential education in the writing classroom and/or how to add more writing activities to an alternative education setting. However, many other disciplines, to which several of the activities or concepts may be useful, are not addressed. Readers should know that with a little creative thinking and effort these activities can be adapted and transformed to meet the needs of other disciplines like art, history, science and so on. When adopting activities, however, the emotional and physical safety of students must always be the most important consideration. Instructors must think carefully and cautiously about all aspects of an activity before employing it in any classroom.

NOTE: All referenced texts are cited according to Modern Language Association (MLA) 2009 Formatting Guidelines.

Chapter One

**Merging Experiential Education
and Writing**

"Either write something worth reading
or do something worth writing."

—Benjamin Franklin

"I never know what I think about something
until I read what I've written on it."

—William Faulkner

While writing and experiential education seem to occupy their own spheres, the links between them are numerous. As a result, experiential education, in its many forms, has picked up on the utility of writing as a central component to the preparation and reflection phases of the experiential learning cycle. Like Faulkner says, writing about an experience or an idea can help an individual truly discover what it is that he thinks about that topic—thus, the use of this skill in educational experiences is paramount. (70-7)

Through relevant thought or theory, this chapter will explore several, but not exhaustive, places where writing and experiential education merge in the classroom and alternative learning environments. While certainly a single chapter cannot cover the entire history of writing or experiential education or discuss the competing ideas surrounding the fields, this chapter aims to provide a broad overview (generally in brief, concise side boxes) to assist educators in using the ideas contained within. The goal of this chapter is to support educators in thinking about how, when and where to use writing in their programming and classes.

Experiential Education and Writing in the Classroom

If it is true that experiences create learning—based on the experiential learning cycle—then isn't the act of writing itself enough of an experience to teach writing? Of course, only through actually writing can writing be learned, but what about the principles of writing? Can writing concepts (like the thesis statement or paper organization) be demonstrated in a way that is less lecture-based and instead integrates different learning styles? Can these concepts be taught in a way that leaves students with longer-lasting information that can be easily recalled? It is indisputable that the act of writing, from in-class writing to writing papers to time in the computer lab, is experiential and is included in all writing and English classrooms. There is, however, room for instruction of many writing concepts to be experiential, or shown instead of simply told (which is also what instructors often ask students to do in their own writing, so the classroom can, and maybe should, be a model of this).

Currently, experiential education is not always commonly used in the writing and/or composition classroom. A student majoring in writing or English may not have any experiential education during his entire undergraduate career. Sometimes, though, an undergraduate English or writing major includes an internship at a literary magazine, publishing house or other writing-oriented profession. This is an excellent way to assist a student in understanding how the material he is learning in the classroom is applicable to a job he may desire. Being in an office and seeing skills from the classroom put to use will help him know if he is on the right path,

The Experiential Learning Cycle was, in part, developed by the philosopher John Dewey and expounded upon by David Kolb in the 1980s. In general, the experiential learning process (Dewey called this the pattern of inquiry) involves four stages that every learner moves through when faced with new experiences or information or when given information that adds to previous experience and knowledge (Evans, Forney and Guido-DiBrito 209; see Figure 1.1 and Figure 1.2). First, a student must have a concrete educative experience. Second, the student will observe and reflect upon that experience. Third, a set of abstractions and generalizations are formed from these observations and reflections. Finally, the student tests those abstractions and generalizations in a new concrete experience to see if they stand up or need to be re-evaluated.

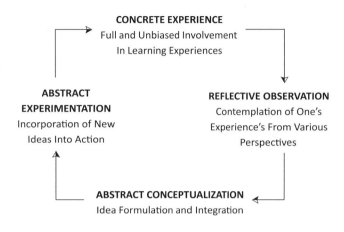

Figure 1.1—Visual Representation of Kolb's Cycle of Learning (Evans, Forney, and Guido-DiBrito 210)

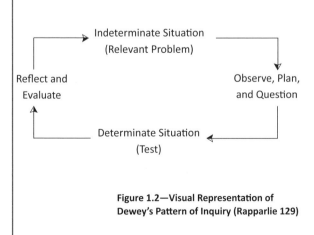

Figure 1.2—Visual Representation of Dewey's Pattern of Inquiry (Rapparlie 129)

These cyclical patterns can happen on many levels for students depending on their background and previous knowledge. Novices to a skill or idea will have a large cycle to help them grasp the task as a whole and smaller cycles within the larger to understand smaller details or concepts. This natural learning pattern agrees with Dewey's assertion that "the ultimate goal of education is to make an experiential continuum where the process of education, that is how a student learns, is given equal footing with the content of education" (Hunt, "Dewey's Philosophical Method," 31). Thus, part of the success of the experiential learning cycle rests with the instructor to align content and process; otherwise, no educational experience can be as effective as Dewey argued it should be.

The idea of teaching through experience is not new; in fact, it harkens back to the teachers of ancient Greece. Socrates argued that "students have something to contribute to the learning and... that the process of becoming educated [is] the important thing, rather than arriving at a final static state" (qtd. in Crosby 6). Plato, who recorded Socrates' conversations, spouted a true belief and interest in teaching through focused inquiry and purposeful experience. In one of his most famous texts, *The Republic*, Plato discusses the ideals and virtues of a city-state, but also explores educational and teaching methods. In order to learn the virtues of a city-state, Plato suggests that people must have life experiences that create maturity and knowledge (Hunt, "Philosophy of Adventure Education," 115). Not once does Plato suggest that learning can come from listening, sitting in a classroom, or reciting facts, but rather that to learn an individual must live what it is that he is trying to learn. Aristotle, a student of Plato, agrees that the foundation of education is based on experience and that the integration of many experiences over time can change knowledge.

learning the information he needs for his future career. Also, this type of experience will introduce him to new information and skill sets (like how to be professional, how to interact with other professionals and within a hierarchy) that he cannot learn in the classroom. On the whole, though, writing classrooms do not offer many other experiential activities than the, sometimes optional, internship or episodic service opportunity. (If you are interested in possible service ideas to integrate into your classroom, consider reviewing chapter 15 of Jim Burke's book *The English Teacher's Companion: A Complete Guide to Classroom, Curriculum, and the Profession, Third Edition*.) I believe there is a place for experiential, or activity-centered, education in the day-to-day writing classroom.

While this text by no means argues for the removal of lecture in entirety from writing classrooms, it does suggest that offering additional modes of instruction, specifically experiential and activity-based, is effective and will provide results. This is based, in part, on research showing that "40 percent of the time during a lecture, students are thinking about something other than what the professor is saying" (Wurdinger 50). If students are only hearing 60 percent of what a lecturer is saying, then they are missing a serious amount of information, which we as instructors should be concerned about. In the case of writing, this is a big deal as no student will face a future void of writing. As a central form of communication in modern society, instructors have a responsibility to do as much as possible to increase information retention and proficiency.

Part of the reason for the lack of attention in a lecture-based classroom may, in part, be due to the fact that many students operate in a manner that is not conducive to the skills or knowledge required in professional or other non-academic settings (Wurdinger 50). For example, students are aware that classes often involve tests or papers and, as such, take notes and study according to what those assessments require. Howev-

to be practiced

er, the working world requires the ability to retain information, think critically and communicate clearly. Writing is a skill used in nearly every profession and students need to master it in order to be successful. Thus, it is the instructor's job to insure that a student does not simply absorb the information in order to spill it thoughtlessly back onto the page, but that he truly understands it and can manipulate it for use in a multitude of situations that may be present in the future.

This kind of thoughtless writing is something I see regularly in my own classroom. One student, who I will call John, was regularly frustrated with his average grades on papers and assignments throughout the semester. He complained that writing was subjective and there was no way he could understand what I wanted or get a good grade in my course, which was his only objective. We agreed to meet for two of my office hours and review his papers to see what he could improve on as the final approached. When I sat down with John, we read sentences and paragraphs from his work aloud and I asked him to tell me, in different words, what they meant. He often responded, "I'm not sure. It just sounded good and you used those words in class discussion." This told me he was writing what he thought I wanted to read, using buzzwords and key phrases without truly understanding what they meant.

We also discussed how writing is like talking to a friend who is learning something new. I asked him to imagine that he was about to make a pot on pottery wheel for the first time and to tell me what kind of questions he would ask. He came up with a list that included: How do I turn the wheel on? How do I control the speed? What shape does the clay start and end in? Does it need to be wet? How much pressure do I use with my hands? These were great questions, I told him, but what if the only information you were given was that you have to press hard with your hands, keep the wheel at medium speed, and have a bowl of water next to you. Is that enough to make the pot, I asked. He said no, he still didn't know how to turn the wheel on.

This was the turning point in my conversation with John. We discussed how it was not only important to consider the meaning of the words you choose when writing, but that it was also necessary to simultaneously think about the order in which you put information. If writing (for academic papers, at least) is about informing other people about topics and information you have researched and thought about, then the language needs to be accessible and purposefully chosen for the audience and the order in which information is covered is logical and straightforward. John focused on this in his next paper and after receiving a much better grade told me, "I never knew writing could be so easy." A year later, he wrote me an email saying that while academic writing still was not his favorite, he had picked up a freelance writing job with a magazine and found that writing served as an outlet for him to communicate to people, organize his thoughts and express himself.

what are all of the dff ways we ask them to write?

This real-life story demonstrates that when students stop thinking about giving instructors "what they want" and start writing with a critical and thoughtful mind, their work becomes a product of their knowledge instead of a regurgitation of information.

Writing to Discover, Communicate and Make Meaning

As with the example of John, students need to understand that the act of writing is not only a way to shape and discover meaning but also an important means of communication. "Putting a thought into symbols means setting it down and letting

To assist students in meaning making and critical thinking, writing is often geared toward communicating or discovering (see Figure 1.3). When using writing to discover, a student learns by answering questions such as: What do I have to say about this topic? What are my thoughts, objections, and questions about these ideas? These questions guide a student to utilize his own language and values in order to satisfy his own need for knowledge (Young 9). Writing to communicate, on the other hand, asks a student to answer questions like: How can I write to tell someone else what I have to say? How can I make someone else understand what I know? This type of writing favors the reader over the author. Regardless of whom the student is writing for, though, writing to discover and writing to communicate both lead to critical and complex thought because often the skills required of each relate (Young 12).

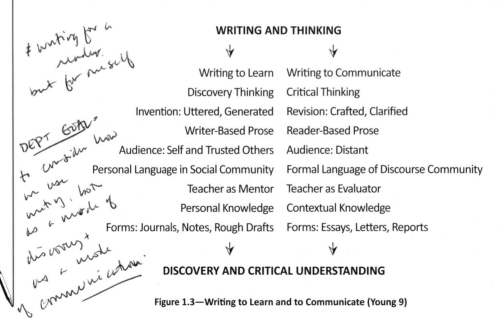

 # writing for a reader. but for myself

DEPT GOAL — to consider how we use writing, both as a mode of discovery + as a mode of communication.

WRITING AND THINKING

Writing to Learn	Writing to Communicate
Discovery Thinking	Critical Thinking
Invention: Uttered, Generated	Revision: Crafted, Clarified
Writer-Based Prose	Reader-Based Prose
Audience: Self and Trusted Others	Audience: Distant
Personal Language in Social Community	Formal Language of Discourse Community
Teacher as Mentor	Teacher as Evaluator
Personal Knowledge	Contextual Knowledge
Forms: Journals, Notes, Rough Drafts	Forms: Essays, Letters, Reports

DISCOVERY AND CRITICAL UNDERSTANDING

Figure 1.3—Writing to Learn and to Communicate (Young 9)

the mind take a rest from it... In this way, [a student] can entertain two thoughts or feelings at the same time or think about the relationship between two thoughts or feelings" (Elbow 55). This balancing and constructing of information is something that humans do from childhood. Early on, we understand that it is only through language that conceptualization of and interaction with the larger world can occur. "Language stabilizes the images of our experience so that they are available to us as points of reference, sources of analogies by which we think" and communicate (Berthoff 111). Thus, language, verbal and written, is the human method of meaning making and expression. Importantly, "written expression is one of our primary means of reflecting on what we think and what we know" (Burke 152). Since meaning making is one of the main sources of how we understand the world, writing can be viewed as not only an important proficiency for school and work, but an essential life skill.

Projects and Metaphors in the Classroom

Since writing has clear application not only in the classroom but also in the professional world and individual learning pursuits, integrating experiences and activities into the classroom can only enhance learning. Wurdinger suggests in his text *Using Experiential Learning in the Classroom: Practical Ideas for All Educators*, that the first consideration when thinking about this is to simply look at how teaching is performed in the classroom. He points out that, "educators don't have time to search out theory for the sake of learning theory. Theory does not drive the learning process, questions and problems do, and information is sought when it is needed" (Wurdinger 52). What he is purporting is that to see the value of experience in the classroom, an instructor only has to see that his students, when using questions to explore problems, grow, change and meet unexpected needs better than when presented with non-problem based assignments. Ruminating on theory, in and of itself, will not help a student know how to adapt to a dynamic, ever-changing world, but actively discovering answers to real-life problems will. Watching how our students learn can carry into our own teaching styles. What students want to learn in class (just like educators in professional development workshops) is not simply intellectual abstractions but rather concrete ways of handling real-world situations applicable to specific fields of interest (situations that many students have not yet experienced and may not even know to anticipate).

One way to meet this need is to have **a question-driven or project-based classroom**. These opportunities allow students to directly engage in the experiential learning cycle and work on projects that move beyond information needed solely

John Dewey's Criteria for Meaningful Educational Experiences

- **The experience must provide further conditions for growth**. Dewey, one of the founding fathers of experiential education, says, "almost everyone has had occasion to look back upon his school days and wonder what has become of the knowledge he was supposed to have amassed during his years of schooling... [it is because] the subject-matter in question was learned in isolation [that] it was put, as it were, in a water-tight compartment" (47-48). Dewey believed that information would be more easily recalled and applied had the information been experienced and clear connections made to other areas of a student's life or knowledge.

- **The experience must be appropriate for the student's level of personal, emotional and social development.** If an experience reaches beyond the student's developmental level, he will feel overwhelmed, self-conscious and unable to integrate information.

- **The experience must not be guided solely by the confines of what the educator hopes the student to learn.** When a student embarks on a project or task of her own volition and explores all possible answers before developing a conclusion, she has then learned a wealth of knowledge and skills, instead of just a single item that the teacher guided her toward. Thus, the education has been greater than a single concept or idea.

- **The experience must provide worthwhile, applicable information that is relevant to the context of the course or situation in which a student is learning.** If a student cannot understand the relevance of an experience to classroom concepts then the experience has added nothing to the student's knowledge (making it defunct). Experience must provide gains, which ties back to Dewey's first point, bringing the criteria full circle.

for a test or paper. These kinds of projects can be essays or research papers where students formulate questions instead of having them provided. Alternatively, a mini-field experience and a post-experience writing project could deepen the primary experience (Wurdinger 54). One real-world example comes from a program called Foxfire that asked its students to collect stories from community members and compile them into a magazine, which was then published and distributed. In activities like these, "the writing project (i.e., books or magazines) drives the learning process and requires students to experience firsthand how to interview and write accurate stories about these people" (Wurdinger 57). Furthermore, when a writing project has a practical use, students generally are more disciplined and focused in their writing. Knowing that an instructor is not the only one who will read a paper and then file it away, often motivates students to put their best into their work. Not only does a project-based learning classroom result in more engagement and learning on the student's part, it is generally more fun for both the student and the instructor.

Beyond project-based opportunities, **classrooms can also be more experiential with the addition of the use of metaphor**.

Many of the lesson plans described later in this text suggest the use of an activity completely unrelated to writing and then propose discussion and questioning that connects that unrelated activity to writing. This is, ultimately, the use of metaphor. The reason using metaphors works is because "metaphor is pervasive in everyday life, not just in language but in thought and action" (Lakoff and Johnson 3). Many times, a person cannot understand something new until she can connect it to something she already can identify. By relating or attaching an experience to something familiar, the experience then becomes less strange and more recognizable. "It is by means of conceptualizing our experiences in this manner that we pick out the 'important' aspects of an experience. And by picking out what is 'important' in the experience, we can categorize the experience, understand it, and remember it" (Lakoff and Johnson 83). Therefore, metaphor can be an incredibly useful way to transmit concepts to students and increase information retention. For example, connecting the idea of sorting through sources during the research process to the sorting of pictures, like in Lesson 17 "Learning to Write a Research Paper," will help students experience how they can begin organizing sources instead of simply hearing an instructor tell them it is a step they will need to complete.

Preparing the Class and Classroom

While projects and metaphors are concrete ways of integrating experiential education into the classroom, there are certain concerns that instructors need to consider before adapting a classroom to include experiential techniques. As discussed earlier, students expect a classroom based on lecture and sitting for long period of time. As a result, an activity-centered classroom often presents a learning environment with which many students are unfamiliar or, at least, are not expecting. As a result, it is an instructor's first priority to prepare students for the kind of classroom/semester/journey the course will require (one helpful resource for educators trying to create a specific type of classroom atmosphere is *Tips and Tools: The Art of Experiential Group Facilitation* by Jennifer Stanchfield). In order to prepare a student for what will be asked of him, the instructor must fully understand how she will operate her classroom. If she decides to run a project in the classroom, she must be able to answer questions like the following:

Do students have the option to do something other than a project; if so, what is it?

Are students all completing the same project, are there options, or is each student's project unique?

Will students work in groups or alone?

How much will the instructor be involved in the process?

How will projects be assessed?

Only with answers to these questions (or questions appropriate to whatever classroom environment that is being cultivated) is curriculum ready to be introduced.

> **Note:** Another useful resource to consider reviewing to help determine answers to these questions is *Teaching for Experiential Learning: Five Approaches that Work* by Scott D. Wurdinger and Julie A. Carlson.)

Once students are presented with course expectations, allow the class a chance to ask questions and voice concerns, perhaps even anonymously. Consider giving note cards to students after explaining the course requirements and ask for questions, concerns, or comments. Then, read the cards aloud and answer the questions or address comments that could say something like: "I don't want to do this," or "Am I guaranteed an A"? Students will be expecting tests and papers. If projects, service or internships will be part of the course, it is essential that they know that and be given the opportunity to opt out of the course or to, at minimum, voice anxieties and have questions answered.

Along with preparing a class for unexpected classroom activities, it is important that as the class progresses, every **student's emotional and physical safety should always be paramount**. Even lesson plans in this book sometimes ask a student to place herself in an uncomfortable position, maybe by being blindfolded or being physically closer than usual to other classmates. It must be the instructor's priority to assist students if they are uncomfortable or outside of a personal risk zone. Generally, the activities outlined in this book require little "real" risk, which can be defined, as the adventure education field uses it, as "the true potential for loss… If no loss occurred, then the real risk was zero. If the person dies, then the real risk was extreme" (Priest 113). However, real risks (environmental hazards, for example) always need to be addressed. For example, do not perform outdoor activities during extreme heat, cold, or severe storms. Minimize all real risk possible.

Real risk, though, is not the only type of risk present. Many individuals will feel what is often referred to as "perceived risk," or risk that a person feels regardless of the actual danger. Perceived risk can often be high when real risk is low or vice a versa. Additionally, **students may feel "emotional risk,"** which is risk associated with personal fears, anxieties, worries and psychological history. For example, one student may find it extremely risky to share a personal story while another may not think twice about it. But, perceived risk and emotional risk are just as dangerous (or can feel that way) as real risk. Pushing a student beyond his tolerance for emotional risk, could shut him down and end any chance that the experience will result in meaningful learning. With this in mind, instructors should give students options during activities; for example: provide different roles that are more comfortable (allow a student to referee a situation instead of participate in it), alter parameters to meet needs (allow a student to interview a family member instead of a stranger) and so on. If the goal is to help a student learn, then that student needs to feel safe but also challenged. While certainly some discomfort and uncertainty are always part of the learning process, extreme levels of those feelings are counterproductive. After considering these concerns about integrating experiences into the classroom, the final step is to pick the appropriate activities for the material and type of learning desired (refer again to John Dewey's criteria for a meaningful educational experience listed on page 8).

Chapter Two
Experiential Education and Writing In Action

"For the things we have to learn before we can do them, we learn by doing them, e.g., men become builders by building and lyre-players by playing the lyre; so too we become just by doing acts, temperate by doing temperate acts, brave by doing brave acts."

—Aristotle

"Learning to write is not a matter of learning the rules that govern the use of the semicolon or the names of sentence structures, nor is it a matter of manipulating words; it is a matter of making meaning, and that is the work of the active mind."

—Ann E. Berthoff

Generally, writing is taught in the traditional classroom with lectures, sentence diagrams and workbooks. While certainly that type of teaching has a place in the instruction of writing, it does not meet the needs of all types of learners and, often, that type of instruction does not resound, long-term, with students. Interactive activities that demonstrate writing principles and concepts create a strong foundation upon which students can stand. Telling a student that the writing process involves pre-writing, drafting and revising is one thing—she hears it and understands it, but may not know how to do it. However, activities that allow a student to think about that process will often help her remember and conceptualize, more accurately and meaningfully, the steps to go through in writing as well as give her time to think about how to manipulate those steps to work best for her as an individual learner. This chapter explains various formats of writing activities. Many of these activities are utilized in the third chapter of this book, but also know that these activities can be used whenever they may be helpful to a concept you are teaching in your classroom or alternative setting.

Placement and Purpose of Activities and Experiences

Part of the work of educators is to develop strong educative experiences that students can relate to the larger world. Peter Beidler, in his article "English in the Treetops," says that, when combining experiential education and writing, "part of [his] job is to arrange experiences through which [his] students will learn enough about themselves or the world around them that they want to tell [him] about in words they find are suddenly easy to write" (41). So, if language (expression through communication, verbal or written) helps us understand and communicate about the world around us, then it certainly can help students contextualize and demonstrate knowledge from educational experiences in the field, in an internship and in a classroom—just as Beidler says his students do. But, simply knowing that language plays a formative role in shaping meaning and understanding is not enough. Instructors must also understand that the timing of when a student writes is nearly just as important. Bynum Pickle suggests that the timing of writing activities has six implications:

1. The place and time in which students produce text impact the text (cognitive, affective, and intuitive place and time).

2. The intersection of time and experience and writing impacts what is written.

3. The intersection of time and experience and social interaction impacts the written product.

4. The physical space in which writing takes place is connected to time.

5. The time or when reflection takes place in relationship to an event impacts the written product.

6. The process of writing takes place in time and across time and is continuously influenced by internal and external processes (194).

These six implications suggest that writing is the result of the intersection of several components from emotions to setting to social interactions. When a text is created and how often it is revisited, for example, are important factors that shape and alter the final product. This also means that writing can be viewed as more than just the exploration of thought (although it certainly is that); it can also be seen as an integral part of the human journey.

Contributing to the "human journey" is part of what education aims to do. Through concrete experiences, instructors attempt to enrich a student's understanding of himself or the world around him. In order to add to this understanding, experiential education commonly uses writing to aid in the preparation, processing, and reflection of experiences. However, students often understand experiential education as one-day ropes course events, a series of service visits, or other brief experiences instead of a mode of learning. The use of writing as a tool to reflect or to process these experiences is also commonly brief or, often times, nonexistent. If writing is utilized, it is generally just before or just after (or both) these episodic experiences. Often guided by prompts, students are asked to write (therefore to think) about their own thoughts on an activity before talking aloud in debrief or a large-group setting. These prompts are regularly general, asking students to answer questions like "how did you feel," "what do you think," or "what does this mean." The benefit to this kind of writing is that students are able to gather their individual thoughts and feelings about an activity before having to share them with others. This allows an experience to have personal meaning before others' opinions and thoughts influence the student in discussion. However, this type of writing (like the experience) is episodic, which often means it does not have resonance. When this is the case, writing is often seen by students as just another part of the activity instead of as a tool to help them figure out their thoughts. While writing does give a student the chance to explore thoughts before talking out loud, the student may fail to recognize that it is, in fact, the writing that is actually aiding in his ability to understand and analyze the experience. As a result, he often does not utilize it outside of this setting to process other life experiences. The rest of this chapter explores ways to use writing as a tool for learning.

Journaling

Now that we know that writing helps create meaning and leads to the greater understanding of all life experiences, in and out of the classroom, showing students that this is true will help them beyond their time in a program or course. Unlike

---

Ideas for Creating Useful and Effective Journals:

- Consider if it is more useful for students to have an open-ended prompt or a guided prompt (this could be visual or written). What skills or insights do you want them to gain from this writing? Craft appropriate prompts or guidelines.

- The journal should "promote fluency of thinking and writing…[serve] as a place to think about a subject to be discussed, a text you are studying, or aspects of your own life…[and promote] experimentation as a means of learning to write or think in new ways without the fear of judgement" (Burke 181).

- Allow journal entries to be "informal" in the sense that students are paying less attention to cosmetic components of writing and more attention to content, their ideas and thoughts. It is also helpful to allow journals to be personalized through words, art and color.

- Offer students a variety of ways to approach their writing including, but not limited to: letters, poems, clusters, lists, questions, stories (personal or fictional), quotations, brainstorming for assignments, explanations, definitions, drawings, sketches, lyrics, observations and/or responses to current events. Permit students to use more than one mode in a single entry. In sum, allow students to think of their journals as "container[s] for selected insights, lines, images, ideas, dreams and fragments of talk gathered from the world around [them]" (Burke 188).

- Consider asking for a specific word or page length that allows students enough space to explore what you want them to, but also asks them to be concise enough that they have to be thoughtful and purposeful with their thoughts and language.

- Tell the students upfront if you will read their journals or not as well as if you will ask them to share their journals with their peers or not and/or allow them to play a role in making this decision.

- Carefully think about how often to assign journal entries and how long students will keep journals (Biedler suggests that more complex thought comes from consistent exposure to this type of writing but too many requirements can be overwhelming or stifling).

- Consider where and when students will write in their journals and how that may shape the final product.

- Decide if revision is important as it may allow students time to reconsider ideas, but only do this if it contributes to educational goals.

---

episodic experiences, programming that occurs over a longer period of time—a semester-long service-based course, a summer internship, or a month-long kayaking trip—can use journals as one way to do this and to support learning. When using journaling, students commonly prepare reflections after each day's events or in response to material reviewed or learned. "Journaling activities ask students to do the following: (1) express their feelings at a given moment; (2) record what they see, hear, smell and touch; or (3) probe the emotional and intellectual significance of their responses to readings, landscapes, people, and experiences" (Brew 3). Writing in a journal forces a student to think deeper about an experience or an aspect of the experience and, generally, the student already knows how to access that writing style, even if it is only viewed as a diary, it is still familiar. Journals "provide students with a space where they can take risks; think differently; and, at times, write more honestly than they could if their thinking were public. The journal also allows a record of their thinking, a sort of road map that charts where they've been and where they are as thinkers, students, and writers" (Burke 181). Additionally, at a young age many children journal or draw to express themselves, so unlike more "traditionally" academic writing, journaling is viewed as approachable and easy, which is oftentimes positive.

As an instructor considering the use of journals, be aware of how you plan to use them and why. For example, if you decide that journals will be collected, know that students regularly temper their writing so they get a good grade or avoid punishment for saying anything "inappropriate." However, on the flip side, reviewing journals insures that students stay focused on the writing task that was provided. When deciding if journals should be collected or not, judge the desired learning outcome. If the goal is simply to encourage more writing than usual or spur thought that will lead to discussion, then collecting journals may deter that outcome. However, if it is necessary to see if the students are understanding material or if you want to respond to students directly (perhaps if working with a particularly at-risk group), then collecting journals may be more valuable than insuring that students feel freedom in writing.

In the article "A Turn Down the Harbor" by Peter Beidler, he relates the story of a class he developed and facilitated at Lehigh University. The basic idea of the course was to teach students about self-reliance by purchasing, remodeling, and selling a local home in conjunction with reading texts on course material (Beidler 24). It was a non-traditional idea posed to a traditional institution, but Beidler was convinced about the links between literature and philosophy, practicality, self-reliance and, ultimately, thinking and doing. Within one week of the opening course registration, the fifteen available student slots were full and the wait-list was forty-five names long. Based on this, it seems that courses that link doing, experience (service, in this case) and academics are obviously popular, but Beidler was concerned about how he was going to assess these students. How would he know if the class was learning about self-reliance and literature through the experiences he provided (which was ultimately how he would determine if the course was successful)? One way, he ascertained, was through journaling. Throughout the semester, the class kept journals of thoughts, experiences, struggles and lessons learned. These journals started off about weather, difficulties with writing, difficulties with learning carpentry skills, and physical aliments resulting from construction work. "As the semester wore on, however, the students began writing about more intellectual and personal aspects [in their journals]—especially the books they were reading and the discussions of them which [the class was] having" (Beidler 29). Journal excerpts that Beidler shares in the article, show the difference in the students over time. Entries later in the semester clearly address powerful emotions and connections between texts (classroom learning) and the real-life experience of remodeling a home, whereas early ones do not. The final reflections the class wrote in the journals say it all—the class learned about self-reliance in an unforgettable way. Had the journals not been assigned for the entire semester, the learning (or at least the ability to communicate that learning) might not have been as marked.

Beidler's conclusions are that journaling leads to complex evaluative thinking, strong comprehension and content knowledge, and the ability for a student to articulate her own ideas and self-direct her learning. In the text *The English Teacher's Companion*, Ken Macrorie says that,

> the conclusion of most teachers and students using [journals] is that [they] get people thinking, they help them test their own experience against the ideas of many others—the authorities they're studying, their teachers, their fellow students. As they become more and more engaged, they often write more clearly, and their journal entries display fewer mistakes in spelling, punctuation, and grammar, although the teachers have taken pains to let them know that they will not be graded on these mechanics of writing" (qtd. in Burke 181).

If it's true that "you can't write and not think," then the more journaling involved in any educational experience, the more long-lasting the lessons will be (Burke 152).

So what does this say about journaling's connection to experiential activities? Students can think ideas through, moving from superficial observations to working through deep emotions and philosophical thoughts if provided with enough time and exposure to writing. "Writing is frozen time, a stop on the journey to tell our story. Thinking of writing as part of our existential journey, our thinking, our lives, and [sic] allows us to further our thinking and learning" (Bynum Pickle 194). Thus, journals provide a literal space for a student to think through ideas and concepts he may not fully understand right away. One of the greatest benefits of a consistent and well-guided journal over the course of a longer experience is that the student begins to develop an understanding about the role that writing can play in his life. Writing transforms from something difficult and frustrating into a mechanism to help process situations, communicate and, ultimately, learn.

Finally, an important note of caution with the use of journals: "The personal nature of student journals raises what is a real concern for some teachers: fear of liability or accusations of violating students' privacy" (Burke 186-7). This cannot be overlooked by any instructor employing a form of writing that can bring sensitive issues to light; instructors need to set straightforward parameters from the get-go. Burke suggests writing an advisory on the initial journal assignment sheet and reviewing it with students to avoid any misunderstandings. The one he uses says,

> A Note About Confidentiality: I encourage you to take risks in your journal writing: write in ways you have not before. Be willing to be honest in your thinking or emotions when you write. I am not saying you should tell me your deepest, darkest secrets. Nor am I telling you to refrain from writing about personal subjects (if you feel the need to do that). But you must realize that the law requires me (and I would want to anyway) to report anyone who tells me that someone is hurting them, they are hurting themselves, or they are harming others (Burke 187).

While you may or may not use this advisory notice, you must clearly state the purpose of the journals to your students. A note like this not only protects you as an educator but also demonstrates that you take the content of your students' writing seriously. On the whole, your students will appreciate this and this commitment to them will also indirectly reinforce the purpose of the journals.

Free Writing

While journaling is one way to help students think about and process information and experiences, free writing is another. Often attributed to Peter Elbow, free writing can be guided or not (3; Hauser and Hanks). If guided, a student is given something to write about, a concept or phrase to spur thinking, and asked to write for a specified number of minutes without concern for grammar. Usually, students are asked to not stop writing for that entire period of time, even if they feel like they have nothing left to say. "Free writing can undo 'the ingrained habit of editing at the same time you are trying to produce.' Most individuals edit what they perceive to be unacceptable as they write. Free writing allows these thoughts to appear and be ac-

- Provide students with a single word, image or object to stir their thoughts.

- If there is a reading or quote that has been used or is particularly applicable, ask students to start writing with the same first line or in the same ilk as the author.

- Do not provide any instruction at all and see where the students take their unprompted thoughts.

- Designate students a set amount of time to write and notify them of the timeline as it nears the end so they can fully complete their thoughts.

- Ask students to write from the perspective of someone or something else that will illuminate concepts you are trying to touch upon in the programming.

- Utilize a specific genre: nonfiction, fiction or poetry.

knowledged" (Brew 3). This kind of writing is useful as a precursor to debriefing or class discussion (reflection) or as a frontloading or brainstorming technique (preparation). It can also assist students in collecting thoughts throughout the experience and seeing how they change over time. Generally, free writing is even less formal than journaling and is not collected or shared, except maybe verbally in large group discussion.

Letter Writing

Free writing and writing in journals, however, is not the only form of writing linked to experiential education. It is common for experiential programs, especially outdoor and adventure programs, to use letter writing in programming (Brew 4). Often, a student is asked to write a letter to herself before a program begins or when it is completed; the instructor then mails them back to the student after a period of time. Other times, letter writing can be used at the beginning and end of a program and then students compare not only the writing but the content of the letter to understand the change and growth that took place. Letters can be written to a parent or other family member. Alternatively, students can write to a future participant, giving advice and reflections to that student before s/he embarks on the same experience. Letters, like journals, are an accessible form of writing for most people, especially since emails are an everyday occurrence. Furthermore, letters are personal and narrative which helps students reflect and create meaning out of an experience. Letter writing during an experiential learning program forces a student to think about the experience she participated in and communicate about it to another person. Most writing in life and business asks people to address specific audiences. Journaling for the self does not touch upon this skill, however, whether students recognize it or not, letter writing does. As addressed in chapter one, writing for a specific reader or audience assists in the development of formal language, contextualizing knowledge, clear communication and critical thinking, all useful skills for students to practice and refine (Young 9).

For example, when teaching an introductory writing course that focused on the theme of warfare, my students were reading Tim O'Brien's *The Things They Carried*. After discussing the text and before writing a formal essay, I asked my students to explore a *TIME* magazine article on things modern day soldiers were carrying with them in Iraq and Afghanistan. Then, in class, we performed a brief free writing exercise on a single item the students were carrying with them that day that was important to them. They were required to describe the item, where it came from, why it was important to them, and how it helped them understand not only O'Brien's story about war but also what soldiers were currently experiencing. My students then turned this free write into a letter that we later mailed directly to soldiers on the front lines. While I did grade the assignment for clear communication, organization and grammar, the assignment also helped students conceptualize and experience something completely foreign to them. There was more revision and care put into that assignment than many of the others that semester. Many of the students' thoughts and reflections from this assignment enhanced their thoughts in later, more formal papers. By uniting two writing activities, free writing (as brainstorming) and letter writing (as practice in writing to an audience and as creating a practical, immediate use for their work), my students were not only better able to understand a text with which we were working but also able to better connect with current events and their own role as citizens.

Clustering

Unlike any of the aforementioned writing activities, clustering is a writing activity that begins with one word. The word should have relevance to the program, the course, or the material being covered. Overall, this activity is best used at the beginning of a unit, at a transitory period in the course, or at a time when an

Ideas for Creating Useful and Effective Letters:

- Return to Bynum Pickle's suggestions on the impact of timing and location when you consider when and where to place letter activities in your programming.

- Consider the outcomes desired from the letter writing; letters for reflection ask for different prompts and timing than letters for preparation, for example.

- Audience—who is this letter going to and why is that important? A letter to a parent will discuss different things than a letter to a future participant or to the self. Inform the students if the letters will be read and by whom or if they are just for themselves.

- Consider if letters can have a direct application or use. Can they be sent to legislators or grantors? Can the letter serve as more than a writing and thinking exercise?

- If you are planning to use the letters for a practical purpose, make that clear. For example, if the letters will be compiled into a yearbook for peers to read at the end of the experience, students may take it more seriously and work diligently on it than if it was just for themselves.

instructor needs to learn what students think about a particular topic or when students need to learn what they think about a topic (Hauser and Hanks). A cluster often helps students not only think about a concept but also about a word and what it means, by denotation and by connotation, to them. Instructors can also reinforce, through clustering, how important words really are and how even though each word has a definition, it also generally comes with attached connotations, emotions and, sometimes, value judgments. From this, students can begin to understand how their everyday words impact others and how they are perceived by others. As such, clustering not only helps students think about an idea or concept but also about language and communication. Furthermore, it helps instructors gain a sense of where students are before they begin an experience or transition between activities (which, again, is why placement and timing of clustering is important).

For example, if a student participated in a single service day at a community garden that existed to provide healthy food to an underprivileged area as well as to teach life skills to inmates from a local prison, students may develop a cluster similar to the one in Figure 2.1. The idea is to morph the cluster from simply a brainstorming tool, which is how many writing classrooms use it, to something that can support students in connecting the experience to the larger world. After completing the cluster, students can write a more formal essay, a letter to an inmate or even a letter to a congressman to reinforce and complicate lessons learned during the service experience. Obviously, this type of clustering activity can be adapted in other ways as well. Another idea is to cluster around an important course concept or task (e.g., analyzing or the writing process or outlining) or a specific time period, event or famous person and so on.

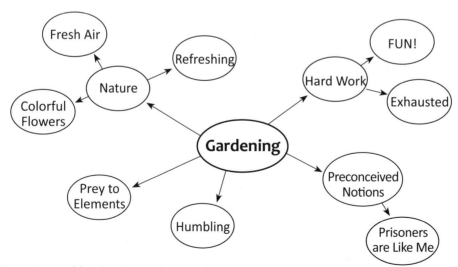

Figure 2.1: An abbreviated example cluster for use in a service experience

Cubing

While clustering asks a student to examine something from only his perspective, cubing is a quick and easy exercise that forces him to examine an object or idea from six or more perspectives by answering a series of questions. Each question asks the student to think about an object or idea in a different way in order to broaden original ideas. Cubing is most useful when working with students on ideas of communication and perception.

Cubing takes twenty to thirty minutes in total (approximately three to five minutes per question) **and can follow these example steps:**

1. Provide students with an object that is associated with an assignment or ask students to take an object of importance to them from their backpacks or pockets—whichever item an instructor chooses depends on the desired outcome (see step three).

2. Have students spend three to five minutes answering each of the following questions:

    a. Describe the object. What do you see? Colors? Shape? Size?

    b. Compare the object to _____. (Have a second object prepared for this step or ask them to compare it to a partner's object. No matter how similar or different objects are, push students to really examine and compare and contrast the objects.)

    c. Associate the object with ideas, popular culture, history, etcetera. What does it make you think of?

    d. Analyze the object. Instead of describing the object, tell how it was made or how it works. If you do not know, make it up or make your best guess.

    e. Apply it. What can you do with it? How can it be used?

    f. Argue for it or against it. If this object were to disappear from the world, argue whether you think that is a good or bad thing.

    g. Sell the object. You own 10,000 of these objects, write an advertisement, poem or create a drawing that might help you sell them.

3. Once the student has completed the above steps, ask her to find a partner and share what she learned about her object and how each question helped her see the object from a new viewpoint. She should walk away with a greater understanding of her object and, ultimately, a focus for an assignment or paper. If

she was working with an object associated to an assignment, she should have a foundation upon which to work. If she was working with an unrelated object, she should be reminded that cubing is an exercise to use at home before she begins writing the formal assignment (Hauser and Hanks).

These questions can be altered to fit a location or event, a specific ropes course element, a piece of science laboratory equipment, the group as an entity and so on.

A. An object that is important to me is a small book, just bigger than the size of my palm. It is green and blue with a decorative, Asian-looking design on the front. Inside, are dozens of blank, white pages that I slowly fill with ideas.

B. It is not similar to my writing implement at all, physically. They don't serve the same function, have the same color or shape or size. However, they do both communicate and I use my writing implement to fill the blank pages of my book.

C. My object makes me think of creativity, moments I've had on the train, in the quiet morning, before bed where I reach, dramatically, for my book to jot down an idea or thought.

D. It was made first by cutting down trees :(grinding the wood into a pulp and pressing it into flat pages. From there, the pages were matched together, bound and cut to size.

E. You can write it in. Throw it at people when you're mad. You can twirl it in your hand when you want to think of a brilliant idea but can't. You can fan the pages in boredom.

F. This book is wonderful! It doesn't hurt your eyes to look at like a neon screen and it preserves the lost art of handwriting. While trees were cut down for its use, you can recycle it and its better for the world than electronics.

G. This book will change your life and for only $10.00! With the ideas you write in it and the inspiring Rumi quotes on some of the pages, you will not only be able to save precious ideas for later use, but you'll also gain enlightenment. This portable, go-anywhere book could make you rich and save your soul.

Student Example of Cubing

Double-Entry Journals

While cubing asks students to examine objects or ideas from multiple perspectives, a double-entry or dialectical journal asks students to think independently about a broad topic, making connections, conclusions and applications, which is often useful in research-based and analytical writing courses (Bean 108; Hauser and Hanks). Double-entry journals require students to record observations in one column and then analyze or think about the significance of that observation in the second column. They have also been called "'access tool[s]' that students can use to hold their thinking. Like sticky notes or highlighting a text, access tools help students slow down as they read and begin to track their thinking" (Tovani 12). Students commonly begin writing without a plan or allow sources to guide and shape their papers instead of their own well-planned, pre-developed thoughts. Double-entry journals can assist them in asking their own focused questions and collecting their thinking in order to guide their learning. While it can be useful to have students write from their own perspective and thoughts like many of the aforementioned activities suggest, rooting students in a text allows writing to become more than just "fiction" from their heads and double-entry journals work well in that way.

Another main function of a double-entry journal is to help a student determine the purpose or significance of specific course- or experience-related material before writing a paper or jumping into an assignment. One example is to have a student enter the quote from a course reading in the first column and in the second column state why he thinks that material is important or useful. He may then be able to interpret the meaning and connect it to an assigned paper or in-class activity. Conflicting quotes could also be noted along with trying to reconcile how that conflict can exist in one text, again resulting in greater understanding before writing a paper. Another option would be to use one column to record a perception the student had at the start of a program, while using the second column to record how she feels about that perception now. Figure 2.2 provides several examples (one per row) of possible ways to use a double-entry journal. It could be confusing to have multiple uses for a double-entry journal, so the best idea is to choose one concept each time.

To take the double-entry journal even further, it is possible to add a third column that can serve one of two different functions. The third column could ask the question: What did you learn from this? This question hones in on student's metacognition, asking him to think about how he thinks, which can increase awareness for him about what he is doing and if the way he is thinking is working for him or not. Alternatively, the third column could also be a column for reflection. Used in this manner, the student completes a double-entry journal at one point in the program, then returns to it after a group discussion to add further notes, additional thoughts, changes in perspective and so forth.

Column One: Observed Fact	Column Two: Significance of Observation
1. Quote from a text that relates to the program	A response to a specific question or guided prompt you want the student to explore, which could include: • So what? • This is important because… • This is interesting or significant because… • I'm wondering… • This reminds me of… • I'm confused and this is how I got unstuck… • The most important part is… • My thinking has changed in this way… • I'm picturing… • I'm inferring… • I'm still unsure about… (Tovani 13)
2. Notes from previous writings or journal entries	Information or observations from the experience that relate to why the student's notes matter
3. Key words or concepts and definitions	The application and/or relevance of the key words or concepts to the program
4. Perceptions from before the experience began	How those perceptions have or have not changed
5. Notes from a previous students who participated in similar experiences	How the notes do or do not apply to current student
6. Lessons learned	How each lesson was learned and how the student will carry that learning with him beyond the program
7. Ask one student to write thoughts about the program	Ask a second student to respond to those thoughts (or do a round-robin)
8. Occurrence from the day that the student thinks is interesting or important	Why the student thinks the occurrence is interesting or important
9. Key moments that made the student think carefully about the experience	The application and/or relevance of the moments to life outside of the program
10. An emotion, event, reaction or quote from a group member or to a text	The learning, reflection on, or importance of that emotion, event, reaction or quote from a group member or text to the student or group

Figure 2.2: Examples of possible uses for double-entry journals

Workshop Writing

Using the workshop model for writing is certainly not a new idea to the field. It is an active model employed in creative writing in beginning levels of education up through the terminal Master of Fine Arts degree programs across the United States. The basic idea is that the majority of learning time is devoted to students talking and thinking together about writing and reading. The actions of reading and writing can often be employed to assist in this process and the same concept can be utilized in any learning environment. While the idea of workshopping is discussed by many experts in various ways, one useful book for the purposes of this text is *That Workshop Book: New Systems and Structure for Classrooms and Read, Write and Think* by Samantha Bennett.

Bennett discusses how the writing workshop is experiential in even its most basic function.

> A workshop has its roots in learning from the dawn of human existence. Once one caveman learned to make fire, he *showed* the next caveman *how*. He didn't say, 'I have fire. Now go make one.' Throughout history, a workshop has been a physical and mental space to organize human learning. Think master and apprentice. Think making things. Think transferring the skills and knowledge from one generation to the next through demonstration and the creation of products that have use in the world—products that help further the course of human progress (Bennett 3-4).

In a learning environment, this means that students are actually doing the learning individually and collaboratively, sleuthing out answers and sharing knowledge.

Workshops "[revolve] around some key ideas: student choice, student voice and ownership, student responsibility for learning, reading, writing and thinking for big chunks of time, and building a community of learners" (Bennett 4). Notice the focus there is not on the teacher, but rather on the student. It is the job of the instructor to merely present concepts and redirect and guide throughout the workshop experience. This not only allows the students to actively engage in the learning, but it also frees the instructor up from lecturing in order to hear and watch where students are progressing and where they need assistance.

Workshops provide a learning experience with structure. They begin with the presentation of a minilesson, students are given the majority of the time to work and problem-solve, then there is a debrief (see Figure 2.3). However, during student worktime instructors should not be idle but rather constantly checking on work groups. When a student or group of students becomes distracted, the instructor should take a few minutes to speak again (Bennett calls this a catch) and

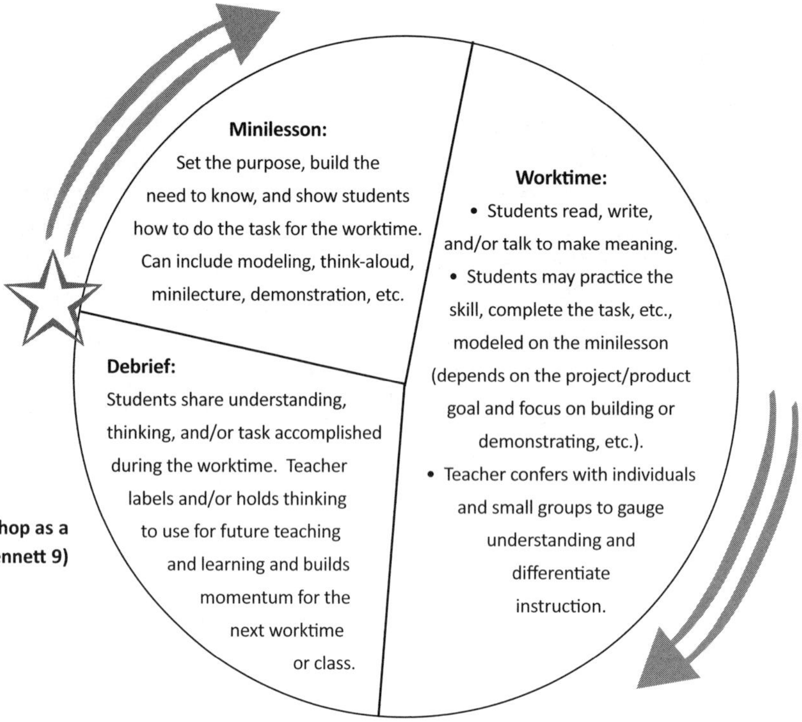

Minilesson:
Set the purpose, build the need to know, and show students how to do the task for the worktime. Can include modeling, think-aloud, minilecture, demonstration, etc.

Worktime:
• Students read, write, and/or talk to make meaning.
• Students may practice the skill, complete the task, etc., modeled on the minilesson (depends on the project/product goal and focus on building or demonstrating, etc.).
• Teacher confers with individuals and small groups to gauge understanding and differentiate instruction.

Debrief:
Students share understanding, thinking, and/or task accomplished during the worktime. Teacher labels and/or holds thinking to use for future teaching and learning and builds momentum for the next worktime or class.

Figure 2.3 Workshop as a Cyclical Structure (Bennett 9)

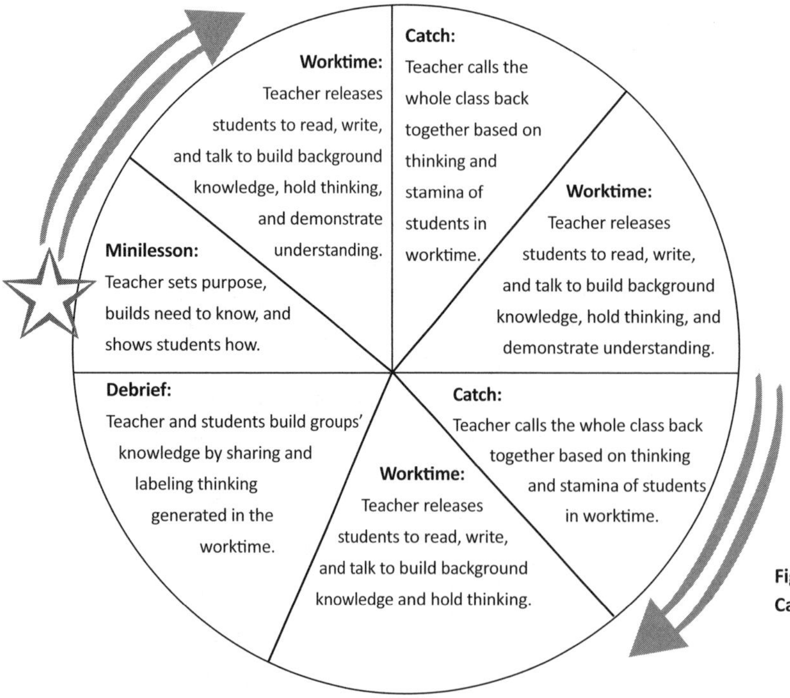

Catch:
Teacher calls the whole class back together based on thinking and stamina of students in worktime.

Worktime:
Teacher releases students to read, write, and talk to build background knowledge, hold thinking, and demonstrate understanding.

Worktime:
Teacher releases students to read, write, and talk to build background knowledge, hold thinking, and demonstrate understanding.

Minilesson:
Teacher sets purpose, builds need to know, and shows students how.

Catch:
Teacher calls the whole class back together based on thinking and stamina of students in worktime.

Debrief:
Teacher and students build groups' knowledge by sharing and labeling thinking generated in the worktime.

Worktime:
Teacher releases students to read, write, and talk to build background knowledge and hold thinking.

Figure 2.4 Workshop as a Cycle of Catch and Release (Bennett 11)

then release them back into work time (see Figure 2.4). This still allows the majority of learning time to be used by students doing the work of reading, writing, talking and thinking.

Of course, as with most of the concepts in this text, workshop could easily be adapted for use in the science classroom (it is very similar to lab work), the math classroom, art, history and other disciplines. It can also be added to several of the lesson plans described later in the book to enrich learning and find a home in an alternative setting.

Concerns and Challenges With Writing Activities

Often, the mere mention of writing can strike fear into students. Regardless of the type of writing activity used, "most people have been conditioned to think of writing as a school task, something that has to be mastered for a grade, and [sic] it is an indication of intelligence" (Bynum Pickle 179). Additionally, each student has a different understanding of the type of writer he is and how successful he is at it. Even an objectively strong writer will call himself "bad at it" because he considers himself to be a weak speller or because the writing process is slow and tedious for him (Bynum Pickle 179; Elbow 12). Furthermore, some students work better with diagrams or pictures and pushing the act of writing can feel constraining.

While many students have an aversion to writing or do not feel good at it, many instructors also carry a set of biases about writing and whether they know it or not, students pick up on them. Since we know that language is connected to creating meaning, and writing (as part of language) assists in the shaping of and reflection on that meaning, writing needs to be seen as an invaluable component of any experience. Instructors need to model appreciation of the craft, regardless of their own feelings toward writing.

Where and When?

As mentioned earlier, the literal place an instructor asks a student to write can alter the type of writing produced or how meaningful the writing is to the experience (Bynum Pickle 194). For example, a loud or chaotic environment may prohibit students from being able to process thoughts and turn them into sentences. In the case of outdoor education, for example, "people's responses seem to be first aesthetic and then later cognitive. In other words, people respond to these [often natural] environments with feelings first and thoughts second" (Bynum Pickle 57). The same applies to the larger field of education, asking a student to write during an experience will force her to focus on feelings or emotions and asking her to write after will ignite more complex, cognitive thought. Only by considering the desired outcome of a writing activity can it then be appropriately placed within an experience. It may, for example, be smart to have students write during and after to make connections between initial feelings and a more detached, processing mind set. To make a decision about where and when writing should occur, an instructor must spend time taking into account the end product as well as the surrounding environment.

How Long?

Not only are the "where" and "when" of writing important, so is the "how long." For episodic experiences, it can be difficult to devote too much time to writing as it encroaches on debriefing and the actual activities being performed. Even during weekend trips, reoccurring experiences or in the classroom, writing can often be difficult to fit into the schedule. Writing takes time and if an instructor really wants a student to think critically about something, the time needs to be given for that. Some students write and process faster than others and, while waiting, get fidgety, thus, creating some anxiety and overall restlessness in the group. As a result, instructors should ask themselves: do I want the group to be together when writing or should we spread out? Do I want to wait until everyone is done (allowing students to think it all the way through on their own time) or give a pre-set time limit (just to get them started in the thinking process)? Answers to these questions help to put parameters around a writing exercise.

Finishing Up?

Once when, where, and how long are thought out, the instructor then needs to consider what to do with the writing that has been completed. Should the group come back together and discuss the writing? Should everyone share? Should only volunteers share? Should there be discussion around the sharing or is the sharing alone enough? These are important questions because they will not only end up shaping a student's understanding of the experience but also, possibly, the way he views the quality of his writing and himself as a writer. If a student knows he will write separately from the group, then come back and be forced to share his work, he may temper or mold what he has written to fit the group's mores. However, if he knows that he only has to share when he wants to, he may write more personal things that are specific to his life but that he wants to remain private—which may allow him to think about the experience in a way that is more personally applicable. One benefit to sharing is that the student may realize how alike he is to others and how he is dealing with similar issues or confusions as the rest of the group. All of these questions point toward issues of sharing, feedback, and trust.

Ultimately, the idea is that these "writing guidelines" need to be developed prior to the experience beginning. It can be a good idea to ask the students to help shape these principles so they meet not only the educational goals of the experience but also the students' needs. Allowing students to participate in this process may also give them a sense of ownership and importance that can be valuable.

Finally, another challenge facing writing is that many students see it as subjective and inconsistent. For example, if a large group attends a team-building session on a ropes course, participants will most likely be split into smaller groups. Maybe one small group utilizes a writing activity while the other uses only group discussion. When the group comes back as a whole, participants have engaged their brains in different ways, some more complex than others. Also, students think quality writing is based only on the instructor's point of view. While certainly style can be subjective, organization, critical thinking and clear communication are not. These issues should be addressed at the beginning of a program or course. In order to be as successful as possible, writing needs to be valued and consistent in use, assessment and application.

Learning More Than Just Writing

Many educators try to focus their classrooms on the student experience and provide educational opportunities that differ from traditional methods (Bynum Pickle 31). The ultimate goal being to "further a writer's learning by exploring the self in order to find better understanding and ultimately connect this understanding to the larger outside world" (Bynum Pickle 32). Regardless of course or program content, this is where the major focus of writing should lie: on how to connect the current experience to larger world ideas (be that a field trip, a themed composition course, a two-month kayaking trip, or an international studies trip). Writing should offer students the chance to explore how the activities, or the process of thinking during the activities, connect to additional concepts or fields of study like: history, politics, society, change, etcetera. By allowing an experience to spur thinking about larger worldly concerns, the experience ends up having more meaning and influence on a person. As a result, the knowledge gained during that experience can be easily recalled (as opposed to knowledge from memorization).

To employ writing activities that will do this, these activities first need to be well thought out. The exercises can be journals, structured prompts, free writing, or a mix, but however writing is used, the type of exercise and what it is trying to accomplish must be purposeful. Second, the location and timing of the writing activities need to be considered. Third, student and instructor biases toward writing need to be confronted and broken down. Finally, and perhaps most importantly, writing must be utilized consistently and assessed objectively to help students make meaning of the events in which they are participating.

Chapter Three
Practical Activities and Lesson Plans

"I cannot teach anybody anything,
I can only make them think."

—Socrates

"One must learn by doing the thing;
for though you think you know it, you
have no certainty, until you try."

—Sophocles

The remainder of this book proposes lesson plans and activities that link experiential education and writing in practice. However, as there is no way to incorporate all possible educational scenarios and settings, these lesson plans should be seen as guides or examples of educational activities. They can be expanded, used in conjunction with other activities or material, or changed to address alternative settings. General instructions—including materials, time, class size, etcetera—are provided as well as some ways to adapt the activity so that it can be used in other courses/disciplines. Instructors are encouraged to alter and transform any of these activities to meet the needs of specific class material and available time.

A Note on Themed and Timed Writing

Two types of common classroom writing activities that were not addressed earlier are those of timed writing and themed writing. Since these concepts can be applied to any activity, it seems apt to address them here. **Timed writing**, while it may stop students in the middle of a thought, asks students to write and to think quickly within a limited amount of time. Thus, this form of writing requires that a student organize her thoughts without being too critical or asking questions like: Is this right? Can I write this? Should I say this? Timed writing is particularly useful in episodic activities or programs where the schedule is tight and writing otherwise would have no place (see Lesson 2 for an example). It can also be used in conjunction with other activities. For example, you can do a timed free-write or timed double-entry journal.

Themed writing, like timed writing, has a specific purpose, asking students to closely examine a specific topic related to the experience. Common themes might be: teambuilding and collaboration, leadership, communication, trust, honesty, learning styles. However, themes can be expanded to whatever is appropriate for the learning environment you are trying to create. Consider using timed or themed writing as an add-on to any of the lesson plans that follow.

Writing Prompts

Early in this chapter, a few writing prompts are given that range from images to quotes to fill in the blanks. Prompts are incredibly helpful to assist students in writing on specific topics. A prompt from one section can easily be adapted to another. For example, one prompt suggests providing the dictionary definition of communication (which mimics clustering). The definition for leadership or teamwork can be used even though it is not listed in that section. Moreover, you could use a similar prompt to explore what students think of thesis statements or outlines. The point is that the prompts and lessons in this chapter can be used as is or can serve as starting points to spur creativity for unique class needs.

Teambuilding and Collaboration

- Some examples of great leadership that I saw today were…

- Collaboration is important because _____.
  I saw collaboration as an essential part of success today when _____.
  I can also see how collaboration will be important to my group after today
  because _____.

- Without a team, I …

- Reflect on this quotation:
  *The way a team plays as a whole determines its success. You may have the
  greatest bunch of individual stars in the world, but if they don't play together,
  the club won't be worth a dime.* ~Babe Ruth

- How does (or doesn't) the image connect to teamwork?

Image courtesy of healthychow.com

Leadership

- Answer the following question: Is leadership telling people what they want to hear or taking people where they need to be?

- Who in history do you admire as a good leader and why?
  Who today demonstrated similar characteristics?
  Did you live up to any of these leadership qualities?

- Reflect on this quotation:
  The price of greatness is responsibility. ~Winston Churchill

- Shackleton, a great explorer and leader, once said that the best qualities a man could have are: loyalty, courage, optimism and chivalry. Do you agree? Why or why not? What other qualities do you think a good leader should possess and why?

Communication

- Communication is…

- I communicated best today when _____.

- Without communication…

- Comment on the Merriam-Webster's online dictionary definition of communication:

    1   an act or instance of transmitting

    2   a: information communicated b: a verbal or written message

    3   a: a process by which information is exchanged between individuals through a common system of symbols, signs, or behavior <the function of pheromones in insect communication>; also: exchange of information b: personal rapport <a lack of communication between old and young persons>

    4   plural a: a system (as of telephones) for communicating b: a system of routes for moving troops, supplies, and vehicles c: personnel engaged in communicating

    5   plural but sing or plural in constr a: a technique for expressing ideas effectively (as in speech) b: the technology of the transmission of information (as by print or telecommunication)

Trust

- Trust is developed by...

- Are you ever surprised by who you trust?
  Where does that surprise come from?
  Were you surprised today?

- The word trust suggests an agreement between more than one party.
  What happens if both parties do not share the same level of trust?
  Why does that happen?

- Does this image represent trust? Why? Why not?

Image courtesy of dailymail.co.uk

Honesty

- If you were asked to create a dictionary definition of honesty what would it be? Why did you develop it the way you did?

- Who is the most honest person you know?
  Why do you consider him or her so?
  Since you find this person honest, does that also mean you admire him or her? Why or why not?

- Some examples of honesty I saw today were when _____.
  Some examples of dishonesty (or incomplete honesty) were when _____.

- Honesty is difficult because...

- How does this image connect to honesty or dishonesty?

Image courtesy of brown.edu

Lesson Plan 1 | Building a Cooperative and Respectful Writing Classroom

Note: Margaret Morrell and Stephanie Capparell's text *Shackleton's Way: Leadership Lessons From the Great Antarctic Explorer* was particularly helpful in developing the "Shackleton Principles" in this lesson. Also, many thanks to Hutch Hutchinson for help with this concept.

Note: While this lesson uses Ernest Shackleton's explorations and adventure to Antarctica to frame activities and discuss concepts, the activities and lesson can be effective, with some adaptation, without the film and the frame. Instructors should not feel obliged or required to use the Shackleton narrative if it does not fit into their curriculum or learning goals.

Materials:
- Film—*Shackleton's Antarctic Adventure: The Greatest Survival Story of All Time* Narrated by Kevin Spacey (40 minutes total)
- Large whiteboard or chalkboard along with appropriate writing utensils
- Pen/pencil and paper for students
- Rubber chicken or other soft, throwable item
- Poly spots (cost between $20-30 for a set of six 12" multi-colored discs) or paper plates
- Piece of rope or webbing

Class Size:
20-30 people

Required Time:
Approximately one and a half hours. The viewing of the entire film adds 40 minutes to the aforementioned time, but it can be done the class period before the activities are facilitated or, if you do not have that much time available, see the activity description for further details on appropriate sections of the film to show and run-time. Also, this activity can be done over several class periods—the required time is listed next to each activity so you can decide how to divide it.

Location:
Indoors or preferably outdoors (a space large enough for students to move around)

Objectives:
- To create a responsible and tolerant writing classroom that encourages positive learning experiences with critical, yet respectful, feedback from peers
- To provide a solid foundation upon which to participate in class

Student Preparation:
Students should read some account of Shackleton's adventure in order to be able to draw upon specific details as they move through the following lesson and prepare to write about it and the learning outcomes for which you are aiming. There are many texts available that discuss Shackleton's journey, but I recommend Endurance: Shackleton's Incredible Voyage by Alfred Lansing. Choose relevant sections to the portions of the lessons you are choosing and have students read the work before you begin the lesson.

A double-entry journal exercise the class session before performing this activity could be helpful as well (see pages 25-26).

Instructor Preparation:
Read the portions of the abovementioned text that you have assigned. Watch and review the Shackleton film in order to know where to stop and start the film for the sections of this activity in which you want to engage. Even if you choose not to show the film, watch it yourself because it is important that you understand and can retell Shackleton's story and the chronology of it (so you may need to watch the film twice). Another resource worth reviewing is *Shackleton's Way: Leadership Lessons from the Great Antarctic Explorer* by Margot Morrell and Stephanie Capparell. While the text is aimed at assisting businesses and corporations with leadership and management, many of the points the book discusses can be applied to the writing classroom and are done so in this lesson plan.

> **Note:** This lesson plan is divided into several activities. You may choose to do only one or two of the activities depending on what you want to accomplish in your classroom. However, it is important not to alter the order in which they are placed. For example, if you decide you cannot do activity two, do not do activity three first and then activity one. Maintain the order listed in this lesson plan. Since part of the objective is to mimic Shackleton's explorations, altering the order would significantly confuse the experience and possibly put students at higher physical or emotional risk since the activities, as designed, build on one another. If you are not using the Shackleton frame, it is still a good idea to maintain this order of activities since one builds on another. Once a single activity is complete, have a short (five to ten minute) conversation about it, not a large debrief. Save the large discussion until the completion of the entire lesson.

Activity One: Preparing the Ship (Mirror Stretching)
—10-15 minutes

This activity parallels the beginning of Shackelton's journey by incorporating some warm-up activities in the same way that Shackelton would stock and prepare his boat for the long journey to Antarctica. Begin by telling the class that's exactly what you're doing: preparing for the class session like Shackelton prepared for his journey.

If you are not using the Shackelton frame, simply mention to students that this activity will help warm them up for subsequent exercises. Also, if there is a reason they cannot participate, offer them the opportunity to opt out or take an alternative role. This is always an option for any of the activities in this book and students should be aware of it.

- Ask the group to stand in a large circle with you in the middle. Explain that to be ready for any journey, the body must be warmed-up and ready for activity, and stretching is an important part of that.

- Begin by doing one stretch, of any kind, and telling the group to mirror you. Hold the stretch for a count of five or ten and then move into the circle with the rest of the group, leaving the middle open.

- Remind the group that Shackelton believed every member of his crew was important, valuable, and had unique knowledge to offer, which is also true of the members of this class. As such, each person will go into the middle of the circle and demonstrate a stretch that the rest of the class will follow. This can be done by going from one person to another around the circle or allowing people to volunteer until each person has demonstrated.

- An option is to have pairs do this (see photos on previous page).

It is worth mentioning to the students, in the beginning, that if there are stretches or movements that they cannot do because of injury or any other reason they should not complete that stretch. Also, ask them to speak to you privately if there are any injuries that you should know about. You may find that some students are uncomfortable with some aspects of the activity. Allow them to join in where they are comfortable and or just observe for a while. Most students will eventually want to join in the fun.

Finally, the point of this activity is not only to begin the sequence of activities in a similar fashion to Shackleton's journey but also to protect student's bodies against injury as the later activities involve more dynamic movement. Also, preparation is an idea essential to writing and parts of the activity may relate to completing homework, pre-writing, being prepared for class, reading other students' work and commenting on it and so on. All of that can be part of the brief discussion after the activity is over.

Activity Two: Maintaining Morale (Australian Baseball)
—10-15 minutes

- Now that students are stretched, divide them into two groups. You can do this several ways: allow them to divide themselves into groups, divide them according to people you want grouped together, have them count off, or ask them to interlace their fingers together (usually half the group has their left thumb on top, the other has the right thumb on top—although occasionally you will need to move from one group to another if they are not equal).

- Once you have two equal groups, show the class the rubber chicken (or other soft, throwable object). Tell them that after they prepared the ship and began the journey, they made it to Antarctica, only to have their ship frozen in the sea. Time is passing slowly and to maintain morale, like Shackleton did, you have devised a game for them to

play and the rubber chicken is the key to it.

• The game requires each team to play a role: one is the chasing team while the other is the throwing team. A team can only earn points when it is the throwing team. One member of the throwing team will throw the rubber chicken. Once the chicken has left that person's hand, the rest of this team's members will form a circle and the thrower will run laps around that circle to score points (you can choose to tell them that a smaller circle means more points or allow them to figure it out on their own). Each time a full lap is completed around the circle, the team should count the lap, yelling out "one!," "two!," and so on. The runner continues trying to score points until the other team (the chasing team) throws the chicken.

• While the throwing team is running laps and scoring points, the chasing team will chase the rubber chicken. The first person to pick it up raises the chicken in the air and the rest of the team members form a straight line behind that person. Once the line begins to form, the person with the raised chicken passes it over his head to the person behind him. That person passes it behind her by passing it through her legs. The passing continues in this fashion—over, under, over, under—until the last member of the group receives the chicken and throws it (see photo). Once that person throws it, the teams have switched roles and now the original throwing team becomes the chasing team and the original chasing team is now trying to earn points.

• Points are cumulative over several rounds. One round consists of each team having the opportunity to play each role. You can allow this game to go on for as many rounds as you like, however, it is a tiring game so five or six rounds is usually adequate (especially if time is limited and there are other activities to follow).

Remind students that the activity involves running and they must be wary of environmental hazards and avoid running into each other. Be sure to point out to them any dips or holes in the landscape. Also, if there are students who cannot run or participate due to injury, ask them to act as referees and/or scorekeepers.

The idea behind this activity is to mirror Shackleton's ideas of maintaining an upbeat attitude, having fun, staying focused, being careful with environment/resources. These principles apply not only to the activity at hand and to Shackleton's adventure, but also to writing. Keep this in mind for the final discussion.

Activity Three: The Ice is Breaking! (Raging River)
—30-40 minutes

The final activity of this lesson is the most complicated, just as Shackleton's journey became more complicated as time went on.

- Provide each student with a poly spot (or paper plate) and ask the entire group to step behind a rope border you have created (webbing, a stick, or masking tape can also be used).

- Tell them the ice has started to break up and they need to get in the life boats to sail to safety. Safety is on the other side (point them to the other border you have laid down—as a rule of thumb, take one, medium-sized pace for every student in the class and then five to ten additionally paces and put the end border there).

- Explain that the space they are standing on is an ice flow and the space on the side of the other border is another ice flow and in between is the swift Antarctic current. The poly spots, thank goodness, float and they can use them as assistance to get across the ocean. However, if they let go of the spot at any time, it will float away, so warn them not to leave the spot unattended. Additionally, they cannot, at any time, step off the spots or that part of their body (foot/hand) will be frozen and unusable.

Facilitator's Role: The group should be able to begin solving the problem; however, keep a close eye on them. Take away any spot that does not have a foot, hand, elbow, or some other body part touching it, even for a second (since that would be all it would take for a current to take away a floating object). The group may only get partially across before it loses too many spots. If more than one third of the spots are lost, consider asking the group to start over since it will become very difficult to complete the activity without enough spots. Another option would be to ask the group to make a choice: continue on with fewer spots or start over with two less than originally provided or with the most vocal person muted or whatever you think might be helpful. An extremely high-functioning group that finishes the activity in seconds might also need more of a challenge—blindfolds (with permission), muting the leader, etc.

Concerns with this activity are, again, to remind the group that if one member is about to fall, he should simply take the step and readjust in order not to hurt himself. Tell students they will not be penalize for this unless the claim is untruthful.

Students will quickly learn to value their resources (which you can eventually connect to valuing each other/each other's work, valuing words, being kind and helpful with peer feedback, etcetera). The aim of this activity is not only to teach the importance of resources (literary, scholarly, in peers, in you as the instructor) but also to demonstrate how to problem-solve difficult tasks (such as how to revise a difficult paragraph or how to find research when it is difficult to discover) and how to adapt to change (losing a spot might be unexpected, but sometimes so is peer feedback or a piece of research or the need to be willing to reorder and so on).

Discussion:

Now, each student needs time to figure out the connections between the activities and writing. Give the students five to ten minutes to develop a list of "Shackelton Principles" (feel free to term these whatever you'd like)—principles that they think Shackelton would live by—this should be done independently. These can include anything they have learned from listening to his story and participating in the activities. Make a list on the board. Some principles might include the following:

- Be exceptional
- Respect others
- Be tolerant
- Be creative
- Be flexible with change and willing to redirect yourself
- Don't give up
- Congratulate yourself on a job well done
- Help create an upbeat environment
- Be meticulous
- Stick through difficult learning periods
- Give constructive feedback to others on performance

Have the students copy this list in entirety onto their paper or in their notebooks. This can be a list that you refer back to at the beginning of peer workshops or when the class seems to be off-track. It is an easy way to remind students what is happening in the classroom, where they want to go, and why they are there. You can even suggest that they move this page to be the first thing they see every time they open their notebooks. Also, if there is time, at the end of the activity or even for homework, invite them to use art materials (colored pencils, markers, glue, etc.) to create a page that has more meaning and feels more permanent and important. This list could be posted in the classroom.

Regardless of what you do with this list, you are asking students to focus on the activity just experienced. The list clearly speaks to behaviors and actions that are appropriate for a classroom. Ask the class questions like:

- Are these principles appropriate for the classroom? Why or why not?

- What behavior do you want to see in the classroom?

- What do you expect from your peers when they read your writing? Are you willing to give that back to them?

- What behaviors modeled in the activities today would you like to see represented in the classroom? Why? Conversely, which would you not like to see and why?

Assessments of Learning:

To assess what students take away from this activity, have them write a letter to the instructor or a journal entry. More formally, students could develop an essay answering the question "What did you learn from Ernest Shackelton/these activities about the classroom and what is expected of you here"?

Lesson Plan 2   Developing a Full Value Contract or Group Behavior Code

Note: Project Adventure developed the idea of the Full Value Contract and has many available resources on their website. Also see Laurie Frank's book *Journey Toward the Caring Classroom: Using Adventure to Create Community in the Classroom* and Chapter 25 of Jim Burke's book *The English Teacher's Companion: A Complete Guide to Classroom, Curriculum, and the Profession, Third Edition* for more information on preparing the classroom and students for interactive and collaborative activities.

Materials:
- Paper and pens/pencils
- Whiteboard, blackboard or easel with large pad of paper

Class Size:
Unlimited

Required Time:
25-45 minutes

Location:
Instructor's choice

Objective:
- To develop a full value contract (or set of principles) at the start of an experience by which the group agrees to abide.

Student Preparation:
Consider having the students read Project Adventure's definition of a Full Value Contract or peruse the website and brainstorm a list of contract items before they come to class. They could also write a "letter to the group" as homework to begin thinking about the actions and behaviors they find important to the group. This could be collected or not.

Instructor Preparation:

Before discussing the activity, it is important to understand the purpose and value of the Full Value Contract to the classroom. Developed by Project Adventure, the Full Value Contract asks all group members to 1) understand and/or create safe and respectful behavioral norms under which it will operate, 2) commit to those norms as a group and 3) accept a shared responsibility for the maintenance of these norms. This kind of agreement is important to all classrooms but especially when curriculum may involve the sharing of personal work, like writing often does. By establishing group norms, students can be held accountable not only by the instructor but also by their peers. Ultimately, this helps cultivate an environment where learning is valued and mistakes are accepted as part of the learning process.

Activity:

This activity is best performed at the beginning of a larger experience with a group that may be together for a longer period of time (anything over a day at minimum).

- Ask students to free write or cluster on the their paper until you tell them to stop (tell them a specific amount of time) a note to the other students in the class addressing their expectations of themselves and of the other students. The final paragraph of this note or a branch of the cluster should be a list of the "non-negotiable" actions or values that each student believes should be followed during the program or course. These non-negotiable items could include: respect my personal stuff, be honest, ask for help, and so on. The list should contain all the items the student believes are essential to have a safe and enjoyable experience.

- Once students have written their notes, ask each person to read his or her note aloud to the entire group. When the student reads the final paragraph with the list of non-negotiable items, write the key words on the board. If another student says the same key word later on, put a tick mark next to the word or phrase.

- After all the students have read the letter, review the list of key words on the board. Ask the group to agree upon ten to twenty key words that every person can unanimously agree to live by during the rest of the experience. The conversation here could get volatile, but keep the students focused and remind the group that this is its first act together and it is important to figure it out since decisions and choices will only get more complicated later.

- Once the groups has agreed on the key words, remove the rest from the board and have the students copy the final set of words onto a fresh sheet of paper (this can be done creatively with glue, scissors, crayons, markers and other artistic materials).

- • Remind the group that this is a contract made by all members. If one person does not abide by a principle, other group members can gently remind that person of the contract principles. Students can "call each other out" and keep each other accountable. Ultimately, this exercise uses writing to help a student think before he acts or speaks. It also develops accountability and group responsibility.

Laurie Frank's book, mentioned in the beginning of this lesson, provides several other ways to craft a Full Value Contract, including a five finger contract (which makes every finger representative of a value so it is visual and easy to remember) and What Do I Need, What Can I Give (81-92). Use her text to build upon this lesson or alter it to fit specific classroom needs or age groups.

Alterations for Other Disciplines/Experiences:
This activity can be used to set classroom dynamics or put any group of people "on the same page."

Lesson Plan 3 | Using the Senses—Identifying Learning Styles

Materials:
- Five notably different objects (detailed in Instructor Preparation)
- Boxes
- Print outs or cards with pictures of a body part that represents each of the five senses

Class Size:
Unlimited

Required Time:
30 minutes

Location:
A space large enough to have five stations far enough apart so a student cannot see what is happening at another station

Objectives:
- To help students use and identify each individual sense
- To show how observation assists in learning and thinking
- To assist students in understanding a personal learning style and its application

No Student Preparation Needed

Instructor Preparation:
Set the five objects and their corresponding body part card in stations far enough apart so students do not have a clear idea what is happening at each station but close enough so you can speak and students at all stations will hear you. If you are working with a large group, you may need multiples of the objects at each station. Each object and station should target a specific sense. Examples of objects that are specific to each sense are:

Sight—colorful scarf, sculpture, painting, photographs, postcards, magazine advertisements

Sound—A quietly playing radio, an instrument such as a drum or xylophone or have students close their eyes and listen to natural noises

Touch—An object with texture (a fleece ball, rock, shell or flowers) in a box with a opening on the side large enough for a hand to fit through but small enough not to see inside

Taste—Candy (M&Ms, Starburst, mints) in a box where a student can reach in but not see inside. You can ask students to close their eyes in order to more easily focus on taste.

Smell—Put something fragrant (potpourri, flowers, herbs, peaches or other fruit) in a box with an opening on the top big enough for a student to stick a nose in, but small enough to not be able to see inside.

Activity:

- Divide the class into five groups and mention that the activity is about using the senses.

- The sense each student will be using will be depicted by a body part card set at each station. Let students know that there may be a note asking them to close their eyes after they have examined the picture with the sense on it. This will help them focus on the sense that is involved.

- Tell the group that they will have five to ten minutes at each station and each student, after exploring the station, should take notes on the experience as it relates to the sense. If the station has a blindfold, the student should write without removing the blindfold, even if it is not neat.

- Then, walk the class to where the stations are set up and put one group at each station.

- Time for five or ten minutes (your choice) then ask for the groups to rotate clockwise. Repeat until each group has been at each of the five stations.

Discussion:

Once the class has completed each station and is gathered together again, ask the students to switch their notes with a partner. The partner should notice which sense has the most detailed notes. He should star that sense and circle the sense with the second best set of descriptions then hand the paper back to the original student. A double-entry journal could also be used here, with the first student's notes in the first column and the second student responding in the second column.

Sense will often tell students how they learn best. For example, if visual description was the most refined or developed, these are students who like to see things written or watch demonstrations to learn. If sound descriptions were really developed, then that student learns best through lecture. There will be students who have equally strong descriptions for visual and sound, so perhaps they learn best by not only hearing a lesson, but by also seeing it written or demonstrated. Some students, though, will have an extremely difficult time describing sounds but an easy time describing touch. These are often hands-on learners that may struggle in lecture-based classrooms.

General discussion, free writing, timed writing or double-entry journals can be used to consider the difficulties of using the different senses and what each student thinks about his or her individual results. Of course this activity is not scientific or a true measure of learning styles, like Meyers-Briggs or other assessment tools which are better suited for a concrete result. Instead, this activity assists students in thinking about their learning style before embarking on a larger learning experience. Explain to students that they may need to ask for something to be demonstrated if they know that it helps them learn. Invite them to take charge of getting the most out of their future learning experiences.

Alterations for Other Disciplines/Experiences:

This activity would be useful to a program integrating creative writing or art, as well as therapeutic settings. Students in these disciplines can benefit from careful attention to the senses.

Lesson Plan 4   Junkyard: Communication, Teamwork, or Trust

Note: Adapted from *Silver Bullets* (Rhonke 24). Material similar to this lesson was published by the author in "How Do We Learn? An Exploration of John Dewey's Pattern of Inquiry" from *Teaching Adventure Education Theory: Best Practices* (Rapparlie 128-134).

Materials:
* Paper and pens/pencils
* Large rope, piece of webbing, or masking tape
* Various objects of different shapes and sizes (i.e., fleece balls, stuffed animals, blocks of wood)
* Blindfolds
* Whiteboard or easel with paper

Class Size:
6-30 students

Required Time:
60-80 minutes

Location:
Area large enough for students to move around and not be hindered by environmental obstructions

Objectives:
* To provide an experience that asks student to communicate in innovative ways
* To develop and create trust between participants
* To demonstrate writing as a tool that assists in shaping and understanding experiences

No Student Preparation Needed

Instructor Preparation:
Prepare the activity by using a piece of long rope, webbing, or masking tape to create a border. It is helpful to begin with a circle or other basic geometric shape.

Keep in mind that there will be several pairs working inside the area at once, and the size of the shape depends on the group size, but as a rule of thumb, the more students in a smaller space, the more difficult the activity will be. Inside the border, toss all the various objects (stuffed animals, fleece balls, wood planks, etc.) so that they are scattered throughout. The more objects inside the border, the more complicated the task will be.

Be aware that during this activity students are asked to blindfold each other and lead each other around. As a consequence, it is important that instructors be aware of anything that might cause slips, trips or falls. Also, be careful to tend to the emotional safety of the students, insuring that they can opt out of being blindfolded if need be. An option might be to just keep their eyes closed.

Note: In traditional terms, as coined by Karl Rhonke, this activity is known as Minefield (24). Over time, language around the activity has changed to remove the association with violence. In this lesson, it is presented as junkyard, as in all the stuff in the border is junk and students should avoid stepping on it. You, however, may want to use a metaphor that is more appropriate for your class and the theme of the course. You can name the activity whatever you want and use the best fitting metaphor for your students. One example is to have the student imagine the set-up before her as an expedition she is about to embark upon. One end of the border represents the trailhead, the other end is the terminus of a successful trip. Her goal is to get her partner from the trailhead to the terminus safely. All the objects in the center of the "expedition," however, are obstacles to safely completing the trip. These obstacles may be events like: bad weather, injuries, food poisoning, snake bites, etc.

Activity/Phase One:

- Ask students to define, on a sheet of paper, the word on which the activity is centered: teamwork, trust, or communication are common, but any word that links actions of the activity with the desired learning will work. Have each student not only define the word but also describe what the word means to her and how it plays a role in her life. Then ask students to put the papers in a pocket or set them aside for later.

- Students should then find a partner. One person in the partner team should be blindfolded. Once that person is blindfolded, he should sit down and wait for his partner to return to get him.

- The instructor should bring the non-blindfolded partners over to the location where the activity is set-up and explain the problem that needs to be solved.

- Emphasize that if the blindfolded partner, while navigating the junkyard, touches any of the junk (objects) or other students, the blindfolded partner must return to the junkyard's entrance and try to cross again—as many times as needed to safely complete the trip. If some pairs finish before others, those students should simply wait until all pairs are finished. Finished groups can, however, remove the blindfolds once finished.

- The most important part of the activity is that the non-blindfolded partner can never touch her blindfolded partner nor can she enter the junkyard (cross over the border) at any point.

Pairs should be provided about fifteen minutes to complete the activity. If the minefield is set in a basic geometric shape, most students will complete the task relatively quickly. Once everyone has completed the first round of the activity, you might provide questions like the following (answers should be done as guided free writing):

- If you were blindfolded, what was it like? If you were not blindfolded, what was it like to guide your partner through this activity?

- For both people, what were the challenges? What was easy?

- What led to your success? If you had to start over, what caused that? How did it change your approach to the activity?

- If you could do the activity again, would you know how to do it better?

Questions can also be focused on specific goals. If you are using the activity to work on communication, questions should be focused on what it was like to try to interpret someone else's words. Similarly, if the focus is on trust or teamwork, additional questions that focus on those topics should be provided. Clustering or double-entry journals could also be used in place of question-based writing.

All questions that are asked should be written on the whiteboard for all students to see and stay up for the remainder of the activity. If a whiteboard or easel is not available, ask students to write down all the questions so they can refer to them as they write.

Activity/Phase Two:

For the second phase of the activity, the instructor should change the border of the junkyard (or, alternatively, two different junkyards could be set up in separate locations before the activity begins). The second junkyard should not be a common geometric shape. A skinny, winding border provides a surprise and challenge to the students who will expect the shape to be basic and easy to master.

- Bring the group back to an area where they cannot see the set up of the activity and have the partners switch so each individual gets the experience of being blindfolded and each gets the experience of being the communicator.

- Again, have the blindfolded partner sit down and wait for her partner to return.

- Take the non-blindfolded students over to the junkyard and explain the rules of the activity. You will need to explain the rules again because this person was not present during the first explanation as he was part of the original blindfolded group.

Allow the pairs up to twenty minutes to finish the second attempt of the activity. Once all pairs have successfully completed the activity, ask students to answer the same questions (or expand on the alternate writing activity you chose) as provided after the first round, but also include questions like the following (again, answers should be done in writing):

- What was easier or more difficult about the second try at this activity?

- Did you carry knowledge from the last attempt with you into the second try? Was it helpful to do that or did it hinder you in any way?

Again, place additional questions you ask on the whiteboard for all students to see and leave them up for the remainder of the activity.

It is a good idea to ask students to write a longer response at this point (several paragraphs) that brings both sections of the activity together. The students should retrieve and examine the slips of paper they wrote at the beginning of the activity. Have them write or cluster about how their definition changed (if it did) now that the activity is complete. Also, have them study their answers to the questions you posed at the end of each section of the activity—this is why it is important to have the questions on display.

Now that the activity is over, ask students if they would change the definitions they wrote before the activity began? Why or why not? Do they have new perspectives? How so?

After giving students the chance to free write, for maybe ten to fifteen minutes, discussion can be opened to the larger group.

Alterations for Other Disciplines/Experiences:

This activity can be adapted around multiple themes (instead of using the metaphor of a junkyard or an expedition, other pertinent metaphors can be employed), as mentioned in the lesson plan. It can also be used more than once during an experience to see how a group has progressed or digressed in a skill set.

Lesson Plan 5   Experiential Double-Entry Journals

Materials:
- Paper
- Pencils/Pens

Class Size:
   Unlimited

Required Time:
   30-45 minutes

Location:
   Instructor's choice

Objectives:
- To improve critical thinking skills through questioning, examining, and exploring an experience
- To improve writing skills and demonstrate that writing is a tool that assists in shaping and understanding experiences

No Student Preparation Needed

Instructor Preparation:
   Review the sections of this text that relate to and discuss double-entry journals on pages 25-26. Also consider reviewing any texts referenced in those pages for more in-depth knowledge. Carefully plan the content of each column of the double-entry journal and how it will relate to the experience.

Activity:
   This activity should be administered at an appropriate time and location for the experience and group. Gather the students, perhaps have them all sit in a circle, and describe the writing activity to them. Tell them to fold their paper in half and draw a line down the crease. Then in the top of the first column have them

write "Observed Fact" and in the second column "Significance of Observation." Either phrase can be changed to something that relates to the activity, the experience, or your particular adaptation of the double-entry journal. Explain to the students what you would like them to write in each column and ask for any questions. For examples, revisit pages 25-26 in chapter two.

Tell students that they have twenty minutes to complete the activity and should try to fill each column, although column two generally contains more writing than column one. Ask them to try to write the entire time, thus making several entries (one entry per row). Have the students write in a group circle or tell them to separate and come back at the end of the time period.

Discussion:

Once all the students have completed the activity, bring the group back together and ask questions like the following:

- Would anyone be willing to share their entries?

- What do you think about other student's entries?

- Did the writing help you think about what we have been doing? Why or why not?

- Did you think about the things you wrote before you wrote them? Or did the writing bring the thoughts out?

- How might writing like this help you during the rest of our experience?

- How can writing help your everyday life? If you do not think it can, why not?

Assessment of Learning:

The answers to the above questions are a true assessment of learning. Instructors can collect the double-entry journals after group discussion, but students should be aware of this ahead of time. To utilize even more writing, ask students to write a letter or a few pages as to how double-entry journals altered their understanding or perception of the experience.

Alterations for Other Disciplines/Experiences:

The doubleentry journal can be adapted to any educational setting as long as the first column always represents a concrete or single item and the second column allows for expansion on that item. In her book *Do I Really Have to Teach Reading? Content Comprehension, Grades 6-12*, Cris Tovani offers several practical examples of how to use double-entry journals to assist in reading comprehension. She also suggests the use of a "quad-entry" journal that an algebra teacher used as a review for a test (Tovani 82). The first column was a property, the second was a diagram of an example of the property, the third was a list of what the student knew about that property and the fourth a list of remaining questions or "what the student didn't know" about the property. This type of adaptation of the double-entry journal demonstrates its versatility across disciplines.

Lesson Plan 6 | Understanding the Importance of the Craft of Writing

Materials:
- Paper
- Pencils/Pens

Class Size:
20-30 people

Required Time:
30 - 45 minutes

Location:
Any

Objectives:
- To convey the relevance of writing to any profession in which students may be interested
- To create an engaged learning environment

Student Preparation:
Ask students to examine a reading about writing that is appropriate for their age group. Some limited options, mostly for older students, include:

- A section of *On Writing: A Memoir of the Craft* by Stephen King
- One of the monthly columns from the magazine *Poets & Writers* about why authors write
- One letter from Rainer Maria Rilke's *Letters to a Young Poet*
- The article "The New Literacy: Stanford Study Finds Richness and Complexity in Students' Writing" by Cynthia Haven in the *Stanford Report's* October 12, 2009 issue

No Instructor Preparation Needed

Activity:

This is a great activity to perform at the beginning of a writing unit or semester/marking period. It helps students work together, get to know one another, as well as discover the relevance of writing to unique goals and interests.

To begin this activity, ask students to take out a piece of paper and, for two or three minutes, make a list of all the professions they are interested in pursuing or to which their majors/interests may apply. Once the time is up, have them circle one profession on of the list they have created that is either the most interesting to them or is the one they hope to make their career.

From here, the students should pretend that they are an employer from the top firm or organization for this profession. They should craft a job description that details the qualifications and responsibilities that this position requires. It is helpful to write the following on the board:

- qualifications (conditions required for job performance—education, experience, etcetera),
- responsibilities (tasks for which employee will be in charge of or held accountable for).

It might also be useful to walk through an example with them. Pick a job they will all know and recognize (like The President of the United States) and help them think of varied responsibilities and qualifications. When reviewing this example with the class, try to move beyond the obvious so they are not only thinking about the "big picture," like the ratification of laws, but also the "details," like giving speeches and hosting parties at the White House. Allow the class fifteen to twenty minutes to create their job descriptions.

When all the students have developed complete job descriptions, ask them to form groups of three and share the job descriptions with each other. Group members should suggest additional responsibilities or qualifications if they think of something the original student did not include.

Discussion:

Once students have shared their job descriptions, ask them to star each responsibility in their job description that involves writing in any way. Then ask students to raise their hand if their job description included writing. Have the students look around the room. Most, if not all, hands should be up. Ask a few of the students to share the responsibilities that required writing. If there were students without their hands up, ask them what profession they chose. Try to get them to think about writing they might have to do in that job. If they cannot figure it out, give them an example of writing that would be required in that job or ask the rest of the class to think of a writing-oriented responsibility for that profession. By the end of the activity, every student should have an understanding of how writing is involved in the position about which they wrote. As a result, it is also worth discussing and providing a sense of how the writing in your class will be applicable to their future. This activity assists in setting up an understanding that work done in the classroom is not "busy work." By beginning the semester or marking/transition period with this activity, you can always refer back to it in order to remind students of the importance of what they are doing.

Assessments of Learning:

For the remainder of the class period, have the students write you a formal letter in which they answer the following questions:

1. Why are you interested in the profession you chose to write about today?

2. Why do you think writing is a useful skill to your future (or why are you still not convinced)?

3. What do you hope to walk away with at the end of this class/program?

4. What do you want me to know about you as a student and learner?

Review these letters and address anything important in a later class or, alternatively, respond to each student individually in a conference or written note.

Alterations for Other Disciplines/Experiences:

This exercise can be used if writing is planned as an integral component of a class in any other discipline.

Lesson Plan 7 | Using Observation to Make Reading and Writing More Accessible

Materials:
- Paper and pens/pencils
- Chalkboard or other projection device

Class Size:
 20-30 people

Required Time:
 30 - 45 minutes

Location:
 Any place with three or more distinctly visual areas (e.g., architecture, ecosystems, exhibits). If you need to remain inside the classroom, small objects, pictures, postcards or advertisements might work for this exercise as well.

Objectives:
- To teach students how to observe
- To indicate the parallels between everyday observation and observation that takes place during reading
- To explain how to use observations, made while reading, in the writing process
- To reduce student apprehension for the reading and writing process

Student Preparation:
 It is helpful to have students review together the concept of free writing before assigning this task (see chapter two).

Instructor Preparation:
 Choose buildings or other physical items (preferably outside the classroom—see location) for students to observe and note. These objects should be complex and unique from one another (they can also be interactive). Having objects or buildings that are distinct from one another allows students to utilize several observational facilities instead of feeling like each set of observations are the same.

Activity:

This activity can be done in many ways; my experience has been to take students on a tour of campus.

- Before beginning, inform students to have their notebooks and writing utensils available, and brief students on what they will be doing.

- Lead students in a walk around campus to see the first of three buildings. Outside each building, they have five minutes during which they should write the entire time. Students should observe everything they can, not only about the building as a structure but also about what is happening around the building. They should try to use all their senses.

- After five minutes—stick to the time limit and encourage those who do not use the entire time to try to write more—the class will then go inside the building and note, for another five minutes, what people are doing there as well as what is physically there.

- Repeat this with the other two buildings. If you are short on time, you can just do the outside of one building, the inside of another or so on.

- If using objects or pictures, allow students to touch, smell (perfume advertisements, for example), look and even imagine sounds.

Note: This activity could also take place in the school building (cafeteria, gym, library, music or art room, etc.), different areas of the school yard, or surrounding neighborhood with a few minor adjustments.

Discussion:

Once back in the classroom, ask the students to break down the steps of what they just did into the very simplest pieces. Ask them what observation involves. They may come up with phrases like: looked around, walked, listened, wrote, observed. Eventually they will realize that observation involves using the senses as well as recording emotional responses. Everything they come up with should be written in list form on the board or through another projection device.

Once they come to understand what observation is, then ask them if this is what they do while they read. Some may see this immediately, others may not. Take the list they developed for the activity and have them develop its counter-part in the reading or writing process. Draw arrows between the two lists to help them see the connections. Although each class will develop a unique set of phrases and words, a possible list may look like this:

Looked around ⤳ Skimmed the text

Listened ⤳ Class discussion about text

Used the senses ⤳Not only saw the words, but interacted with the text through active and critical reading

Emotional response ⤳ Noted where I agreed and disagreed, was confused, or had additional questions or I actually felt something in response to what I was reading

By developing this list, students should be able to see that reading and writing are as accessible as walking around and looking at everyday objects (which is the power of observation all of them already know how to perform). By making texts seem more approachable, students may be less fearful of the studies ahead of them.

Assessment of Learning:

Have students write a single paragraph response to the activity. It could be a free write about what they learned or a more formal paragraph where they use the observations they made to write a paragraph that answers a question like: What is the role of (insert building name) at (insert campus/school name)?

Alterations for Other Disciplines/Experiences:

This activity is useful in any discipline where reading will be a major part of a course. It is especially helpful in remedial courses. This activity could also be useful in alternate settings if the program will involve a lot of reading and writing. Remember that students are often hesitant or have a set of biases or preconceived notions about their abilities as readers and writers, so this activity could be extremely useful and used as a reference point later on in programming.

Lesson Plan 8 | Developing Principles to Support the Writing Process

Note: Margaret Morrell and Stephanie Capparell's text *Shackelton's Way: Leadership Lessons From the Great Antarctic Explorer* was particularly helpful in developing the "Shackleton Principles" in this lesson. Also, many thanks to Hutch Hutchinson for help with this concept.

Note: While this lesson uses Ernest Shackelton's explorations and adventure to Antarctica to frame activities and discuss concepts, the activities and lesson can be effective, with some adaptation, without the film and the frame. Instructors should not feel obliged or required to use the Shackleton narrative if it does not fit into their curriculum or learning goals.

Materials:

- Film—*Shackelton's Antarctic Adventure: The Greatest Survival Story of All Time* Narrated by Kevin Spacey (40 minutes total)
- Large whiteboard or chalkboard along with appropriate writing utensils
- Pen/pencil and paper for students
- Four cones or other boundary markers
- Two swimming noodles
- Various throwable items
- A length of rope or webbing
- A platform or carpet square

Class Size:

20-30 people

Required Time:

Approximately one hour. The viewing of the entire film adds 40 minutes to the above-mentioned time, but it can be done the class period before the activities are facilitated or, if you do not have that much time available, see the activity description for further details on appropriate sections of the film to show and run-time. Also, this activity can be done over several class periods so the required time is listed next to each activity in both parts so you can decide how you might be able to divide it.

Location:

Indoors or preferably outdoors (enough space for students to move around)

Objectives:

- To create a concrete activity/metaphor to explain and demonstrate the steps in the writing process
- To demonstrate to students how to be resourceful both in writing and outside of writing
- To help students think about themselves as writers

Student Preparation:

Students should read some account of Shackleton's adventure in order to be able to draw upon specific details as they move through the this lesson and prepare to write about it and the learning outcomes for which you are aiming. There are many texts available that discuss Shackleton's journey, but I recommend *Endurance: Shackleton's Incredible Voyage* by Alfred Lansing. Choose relevant sections to the portions of the lessons you are choosing and have students read the work before you begin the lesson.

A double-entry journal exercise in the class session before performing this activity could be helpful as well.

Instructor Preparation:

Read the portions of the abovementioned text that you have assigned. Watch and review the Shackelton film in order to know where to stop and start the film for the sections of this activity in which you want to engage. Even if you choose not to show the film, watch it yourself because it is important that you understand and can retell Shackelton's story and the chronology of it (so you may need to watch the film twice). Another resource worth reviewing is *Shackelton's Way: Leadership Lessons from the Great Antarctic Explorer* by Margot Morrell and Stephanie Capparell. While the text is aimed at assisting businesses and corporations with leadership and management, many of the points the book discusses can be applied to the writing classroom and are done so in this lesson plan.

> **Note:** This lesson plan is divided into several activities. You may choose to do only one or two of the activities depending on what you want to accomplish in your classroom. However, it is important not to alter the order in which they are placed. For example, if you decide you cannot do activity two, do not do activity three first and then activity one. Maintain the order listed in this lesson plan. Since part of the objective is to mimic Shackleton's explorations, altering the order would significantly confuse the experience and possibly put students at higher physical or emotional risk since the activities, as designed, build on one another. If you are not using the Shackleton frame, it is still a good idea to maintain this order of activities since one builds on another. Once a single activity is complete, have a short (five

to ten minute) conversation about it, not a large debrief. Save the large discussion until the completion of the entire lesson.

Activity One: Gathering the Crew (Blob Tag)
—10 minutes

- Set up a boundary area using the four cones. Pace out the number of students for each side of your square, so 20 students is a 20 x 20 square.

- Ask for two student volunteers and tell them they are the only members of your crew that you can find, but there is a big task ahead and the whole group needs to reconvene. Give each volunteer a swimming noodle and tell them to round up the rest of the crew.

- The volunteers must join hands and gather the rest of the crew by tapping them with the noodles. The rest of the crew wants to stay outside and play so they should try to avoid the "taggers." They cannot run outside of the four cone boundary.

- When a crew member gets tagged, they have to join the taggers by joining hands with them in the middle.

- Remind the group to be cautious of any environmental hazards that would cause trips or falls. Ask the taggers to be careful with how hard and where they hit other group members, absolutely avoiding the face and genitals.

- By the end the entire crew should be linked in one long line, ready for the next activity.

Activity Two: Sailing to Safety (Junkyard)
—20-30 minutes

This second activity is designed to mimic Shackleton's dangerous and long sail toward the wailing station. See the Lesson Plan entitled "Junkyard: Communication, Teamwork, or Trust" for the set up and description of junkyard.

Instead of guiding discussion after this activity toward the research process, guide students toward thoughts on the writing process—brainstorming, writing and revision. Also consider attention to details, like that which is required for grammar, structure and organization of a paper. Feel free to branch out into ideas of peer review (how the students were assisting and relying on each other) and rewriting (if they had to start over or just how they sometimes had to ask questions because they didn't hear it correctly the first time).

Activity Three: Rescuing the Crew (All Aboard)
—15-25 minutes

Walk the students to a platform set in an open area. These are generally wooden, platforms about 3" to 10" off the ground and dimensions vary, based on the size of the group, from 1' x 1' to 3.5' x 3.5'. If you have access to a ropes course, you can use the All Aboard platform if installed there, otherwise you can create the platform size out of a piece of old rug or something stiff enough so that the borders cannot be altered, flipped or ripped by people stepping on it.

Bring in Shackelton's story by reminding students that the Boss has just made it to the whaling station and has returned to rescue them. This is an exciting day, but they all need to fit on the rescue boat, which is in front of them. Whatever happens, the Boss will not leave anyone behind so they have to figure out how everyone can fit without falling off. To determine successful rescue, every group member needs to have all her limbs and body on the platform and, together, the group must sing "Row, Row, Row Your Boat" two times without anyone stepping off the platform. Only then have they reached safety.

> Note: If someone is about to fall off the platform, they should simply step off and rebalance instead of falling down, hurting themselves or pulling the entire group off the platform with them.

This activity aims at getting students to think about their final product, being proud of what they turn in as well as giving credit to the appropriate authors (acknowledging that the whole group was part of the success not just the individual).

Discussion:

Each student needs time to figure out the connections between the activities and writing. Give the students five to ten minutes to develop a list of "Shackelton principles" (feel free to term these whatever you'd like)—principles they think Shackelton would live by—this should be done independently. These can include anything they have learned from listening to his story and participating in the activities. Put the list on the board and feel free to add to the list principles that the group does not think of or other items that you (or a student) come up with that are not listed below.

You want students to develop a list that includes the following:

- Be flexible with change and willing to redirect yourself.
- Use the best tools/resources available.
- Connect to your interests.
- Know your stuff.
- Stick through difficult learning periods.
- Learn new skills.
- Learn from mistakes.
- Focus on a central vision.
- Give feedback to others on performance.
- Divide big projects into pieces.
- Don't cut corners, it leads to mistakes.

Have the students copy this list in entirety onto their paper or in their notebooks. This can be a list that you refer back to at the beginning of peer workshops or when the class seems to be off-track. It is an easy way to remind students of what is happening in the classroom, where they want to go, and why they are there. Suggest that they move this page to a prominent place in their notebooks. Also, if there is time, at the end of the activity or even for homework, invite them to use art materials (colored pencils, markers, glue, etc.) to create a page that has more meaning and feels more permanent. Regardless of what you do with this list, you are asking students to focus on the activity just experienced. The list clearly speaks to principles that guide the writing process. Ask the class questions like the following:

- Do you get frustrated with writing? Why or why not? If so, what will you do to refocus yourself as you work this semester/marking period?

- How do the activities today represent or symbolize the writing process? (Name each activity when asking this so it is easy for students to visualize.)

- Is it important to celebrate success in writing?

- What can we learn from Shackelton about our attitudes toward writing?

Assessments of Learning:

To assess what students took away from the activities of this lesson, have them write a letter to the instructor or write a journal entry. More formally, a student could develop an essay or free write answering the question "What did you learn from Ernest Shackelton about the writing process"? This could be used to start discussion at the beginning of the next class.

Alterations for Other Disciplines/Experiences:

Review the book *Make Me a Story: Teaching Writing Through Digital Storytelling* by Lisa Miller for ideas on how to take this experience and transform it into a writing opportunity that engages with technology. This would be an excellent idea for a computer literacy course, a keyboard course or any course linking the use of technology with reading and writing.

Lesson Plan 9 | How to Organize an Essay

Note: Also see Lesson 20 for another suggestion on how to show students how to organize an essay, especially if all the props in this lesson would prove problematic. Another way to teach this would be to use the Zoom exercise from Lesson 17, but to focus on organization of a paper instead of research throughout the activity.

Materials:
- Two complete, matching sets of various items (e.g., boards, stackable items, rope, balls)
- Two pieces of rope, webbing, sticks or masking tape (to create a border)
- Three blindfolds
- Pens/pencils and paper

Class Size:
Ideally, this exercise would be performed with nine students, however, if the class is larger break students into groups of about nine students (this can vary slightly but generally increases should be in multiples of three if possible) and double the materials listed above for each set of nine students.

Required Time:
Approximately 60 minutes (depending on the complexity of the structure)

Location:
Indoors or outdoors (enough space for students to move around)

Objectives:
- To teach students how to think about the organization of a paper
- To create camaraderie between students

No Student Preparation Needed

Instructor Preparation:
Create a structure out of one set of the items available and place a piece of rope, webbing, stick or masking tape in front of the items as a border. Take the second

set of materials and put them about twenty to thirty paces in one direction from the structure. Take another twenty to thirty paces in the other direction and place a second border with a piece of rope or webbing.

Activity:

- Have students gather in the area where the activity will be completed with their backs facing the structure you previously built. Ask for three volunteers to be the engineers.

- Tell the engineers that they need to choose three people who will be builders and three people who will be communicators.

- The communicators should go to the far border (with their backs still facing the structure). The builders should stand next to the pile of materials in the middle and put on blindfolds.

- The only students who should be able to see the structure are the engineers. Tell the engineers that they cannot speak, but that the communicators and builders can. Since the engineers are the only ones who can see the structure, they have to describe, non-verbally, to the communicators how to build the structure. The communicators will then pass that information to the builders, who will arrange the pieces in the middle into a replica of the structure (see photo for setup).

Generally, the students form groups of three with one engineer, communicator and builder working as a team, which means three complete teams in the group trying to work together to rebuild the structure. Be very aware of how the builders are moving materials around, however. Because they cannot see each other, instructors are responsible for their physical safety. If there are additional students, this can be a job assigned to them.

The idea is to ultimately connect this activity to the organization of an essay so pay attention to how carefully students put pieces together, what they say, how they communicate, the specific language and body language they use and so on. This may be useful in the final discussion.

Discussion:

Once the activity is over, ask the students to take a pen and paper and sketch (for just a few minutes) the final structure and the original structure as well as make notes on differences and similarities. Each student should bring the sketches to the large circle for discussion.

Begin the discussion with general questions like:

- What was it like to be stuck in the role you were given? Were you frustrated? Were there parts that were easier than others—what were they?

- How successful was your final product in duplicating the original structure?

- What do you think went wrong? Did you ever want to give up? Why?

- What was the easiest part? Why do you think that was so?

Then move the discussion to connect the activity to writing. Some questions that might be asked are:

- If communication was a problem in getting the structure to look like the original, what can that mean for us as writers?

- The final product did not look exactly like the engineers intended, so it would be confusing to someone who was expecting to see the original. How can we relate this to how we structure papers?

- The final product looked exactly like the original so nothing was confusing or strange. How can we relate to this to how we structure papers?

- Why is it important to think about how we organize a paper in the same way it was important to think about how you placed each piece when rebuilding the structure?

- Consider connecting specific dialogue or actions from the students during the activity to the structuring of a paper.

The class should begin to understand that each piece in the structure had an appropriate place, just the way information in an essay has an appropriate place. For example, if the first body paragraph (which should be foundational information that is built upon in the rest of the essay) contains complex details that should really be in the third body paragraph, it is confusing to the reader. For example, if an important piece of the base of the structure was mislaid or, if a small piece was in the wrong place, it is like a detail written in the wrong part of an essay. It does not look right or it is not as was intended so the reader may get the wrong message. Also, you want students to think about how, if they are unsure how to structure an essay in the beginning, it will show in the final product—just like if the engineers were not clear in their communication.

Assessment of Learning:

Ask for a written paragraph where the students summarize what they learned from the activity and collect it before class is over. For a more formal assignment, have the students write a one- or two-page response to the activity. Another option is to require a written paragraph on how each student thinks he or she approaches writing and how this activity has changed (or not changed) his or her thinking about that process.

Alterations for Other Disciplines/Experiences:

This activity can also be used to work on teamwork or communication. In other academic disciplines, this could helpful for classes that deal with putting events together, like history, or perhaps shop classes or home economics.

Lesson Plan 10 ✏ Working on Clarity

Thanks to Nicole Kenley for sharing this worksheet with me.

Materials:
- Copies of the handout provided at the end of this lesson plan
- Pens/pencils

Class Size:
Any

Required Time:
20-30 minutes

Location:
Classroom or other area where students can easily write on a hard surface

Objectives:
- To illustrate the value of being clear when writing or communicating
- To demonstrate the importance of sentence structure and word choice as essential components of clarity
- To encourage students to find value and learning in making mistakes (their own or others)

Student Preparation:
Bring a recently graded or drafted paper to class.

Instructor Preparation:
Review the handout at the end of this lesson and insure that it is appropriate for your students. Remove any material you don't want to include and copy the handout, one per student (even if you decide to have them work in pairs or teams).

Activity:

A common issue that students face in writing and verbal communication is that of clarity. I often find, when sitting down with students over drafted essays, that when I ask them to explain a sentence I find difficult to understand in their own words, they are more eloquent than they were on the page. When I ask them why they didn't just write what they said aloud, they tell me they didn't think that was allowed. There seems to be a common perception that complex sentences and big words trump clear, straightforward communication. This simply isn't so.

Begin this activity by providing each student with a copy of the handout found at the end of this exercise. If there are any headlines that you want removed from the exercise due to their content or due to time constraints, feel free to remove them. Also, consider if you want to copy the third page, which works as an assessment piece for the end of the activity, but also adds approximately ten to fifteen minutes of writing time to the activity.

Tell the students that there is something wrong with each of the headlines on the handout, that they don't say what the author originally intended. They should (as individuals, pairs or groups—your choice) write a new sentence (not a headline) beneath the incorrect one that says what they assume to be the author's original intent. This is detailed in the paragraph of directions at the top of the handout, so you should read this aloud to them and ask them to follow along. Remind them that mistakes happen, we all mess up when we write sometimes, but that it's important to remember to laugh at our mistakes, when appropriate, and learn from them. Allow them approximately ten to fifteen minutes to complete the worksheet. Walk around the room to see if they are questions about any of the "hidden meanings" in the headlines.

Discussion:

Once the worksheets are completed, have a few volunteers read the headlines they liked the most as well as their corrected sentences. If you put the students in groups, have each group share one or two headlines. Then, consider asking them the following questions:

- What issues does this activity bring up for us to consider about our own writing?

- Should we be concerned about the many ways readers could take what we write? Why or why not?

- Would you put your name to any of these headlines? Why or why not?

- How does clarity factor into this exercise?

- If you had to name one thing this activity taught you, what would it be?

Assessment of Learning:

At the end of the worksheet, there are two assessment options, Part I and Part II. Choose the one that best suits your class needs, or make up another one that addresses a specific learning objective you had for this lesson.

Another assessment of learning is to ask students to review and revise the recently graded or drafted paper that they were asked to bring with them to this class session. They should take around fifteen to twenty minutes and note places where their paper could be clearer.

Neither assessment listed here is included in the estimated time noted in this lesson plan, but instead, these assessments would be in addition to the time mentioned at the beginning of the lesson or should be completed as homework.

Alterations for Other Disciplines/Experiences:

This activity would be great for a journalism, public speaking, debate or communications course. It also works well in basic writing courses or with younger students, although some younger students may miss the "hidden meaning" in a few of the headlines so consider going over the first two or three together as a large group.

Working on Clarity

All of these are real headlines found in newspapers across the nation. There's something wrong, though. They do not say what they actually mean! In the space beneath the headline, write a new sentence (not necessarily a headline) that conveys what you think the original author was trying to say. Don't forget to laugh! We all make mistakes and what originally makes sense to us can be funny to others. What is important is that we learn from our mistakes and those of others, so let's start by learning from these mistakes in order to improve our own work.

1. Grandmother of Eight Makes Hole in One

2. Deaf Mute Gets New Hearing in Killing

3. William Kelly was Fed Secretary

4. Milk Drinkers are Turning to Powder

5. Iraqi Head Seeks Arms

6. Prostitutes Appeal to Pope

7. Panda Mating Fails—Veterinarian Takes Over

8. NJ Judge to Rule on Nude Beach

9. Dealers Will Hear Car Talk at Noon

10. Miners Refuse to Work After Death

11. Two Soviet Ships Collide—One Dies

12. Autos Killing 110 a Day, Let's Resolve to Do Better

13. Blind Woman Gets New Kidney From Dad She Hasn't Seen in Years

14. Death Causes Loneliness, Feeling of Isolation

Working on Clarity

PART I: Once you've completed this worksheet, use the rest of this sheet of paper to write a paragraph to your instructor that explains what you learned from this activity and how you can apply it to your own writing.

PART II: Choose two of the above headlines and instead of writing a sentence stating what you think the author intended, write a new headline (which needs to be attention-grabbing and informative). Under each revision write four to six sentences describing why you made the changes you made and how you think the changes make the headline more clear to the reader.

Lesson Plan 11 ✏ Word Choice

Materials:
- Copies of the handout provided at the end of this lesson plan
- Pens/pencils

Class Size:
Any

Required Time:
20-25 minutes

Location:
Classroom or other area where students can easily write on a hard surface

Objectives:
- To understand the importance of word choice in writing and communication
- To consider what words mean by their denotations and connotations
- To realize how the words used in writing can create an overall tone to an essay or create an impression on the reader

No Student Preparation Needed

Instructor Preparation:
Make copies of the handout at the end of this activity, one for each student, or write the words in column one on the board or large pieces of paper to display.

Activity:
Briefly talk to the students about word choice and why you think it is important in writing and communication as a whole. Alternatively, you could ask the students to cluster around two words (examples could be: terrorist and religious fundamentalist, or prison and incarceration, or punishment and time out, or take one example from the worksheet). Discuss the clusters and relate them to the idea of connotation and denotation and the fact that every word has both. Tell

the students, as they consider each word or phrase on the worksheet, to also think about both the literal and hidden meaning of each word during the comparison. Then, either give them the worksheet and read the directions aloud or show them the words by holding up cards that have both words written on them or by writing the paired words on the board.

Discussion:

Ask a few students to share what they wrote in column two. Then, proceed with group discussion that explores questions like the following:

- What was it like trying to think carefully about these associations? Did any of these comparisons make you uncomfortable? Which one(s) and why or why not?

- Is word choice only important for nouns and descriptors like the ones on this sheet? If no, when else is it important to consider word choice and why?

- The top of the worksheet asks some pointed questions, let's talk about each one in detail. Refer to any of the examples on the worksheet to illustrate your thoughts.

- How can we apply the concepts we've talked about today regarding word choice to our own writing?

Assessment of Learning:

For homework, ask students to choose one comparison from the worksheet to compare further. They should formally look up dictionary definitions of each word and type each phrase into Google or another search engine to see what comes up. They can ask family members or other students for their thoughts on each word. They should prepare a one to two page informal response (meaning it will not be graded for cosmetic components) that discusses the two words in depth and ends with a final paragraph that describes the student's own thoughts on the importance of word choice in writing.

Alterations for Other Disciplines/Experiences:

For this activity, column one can be changed to fit any experience that students are about to embark upon. For example, if students are about to begin a service experience working with men and women from a local prison, all the words in column one could relate to that (ex-convict versus rehabilitated citizen, criminal vs. inmate, service-learning vs. volunteer, giving back vs. charity and so on). This activity can be helpful not only with word choice but also with exploring preconceived notions, biases and so on.

Word Choice

To complete this handout, you must fill in column two by comparing the words in column one. Answer the following questions for each comparison:

- How does the word have different effect reader?
- What does the word suggest? What associations are made with that word?
- What does the word reveal about the author's position on the subject?

Column One	Column Two
Retarded versus Mentally Disabled	
Insane Asylum versus Mental Hospital	
Healthy Forest Initiative versus Slash and Burn Agriculture	
Wheelchair Bound versus Wheelchair User	
Performance Enhancing Drug versus Steroid	
Cancer Survivor versus Cancer Victim	
War Hero versus War Veteran	
Drug User versus Drug Addict	
Gay versus Homosexual	

© 2011 Writing and Experiential Education, Wood 'N' Barnes Publishing

Lesson Plan 12 | Writing a Thesis, Lesson One

Note: Adapted from *Silver Bullets* (Rhonke 100)

Materials:
None

Class Size:
Unlimited

Required Time:
15-20 minutes

Location:
Indoors or outdoors (a space that is large enough for students to move around)

Objective:
• To help students conceptualize the pieces of a thesis statement

No Student Preparation Needed

Instructor Preparation:
Provide students with the handout "Two Models of Thesis Writing" on page 90.

Activity:
Place student in pairs and ask them to sit facing one another so the bottoms of their feet are touching, knees bent, and hands tightly grasped (this exercise is best suited for students of about the same physical size). Do not allow interlocking arms as that could result

in shoulder injury. The goal is for the students to pull themselves up to the standing position without moving their feet. Once a pair has completed the activity, ask a group of three to try, then four, then five, until the entire class tries at the end.

The criteria for success in this activity is:

• Hands remain grasped, as though an electrical current could pass through all group members

• Feet touch, as though an electrical current could pass through all group members

• Group members rise at the same time (butts off the ground together)

The group will find it difficult to have more than eight students in the circular configuration to stand. Try to push them to be innovative in thinking. If a large group is able to raise all people off the ground only a few inches and the group is proud of that accomplishment, it is up to the instructor to call that a success or not, but think about why "yes" and why "no."

Discussion:

Begin discussion by asking general questions:

• What was easy or difficult about this activity?

• Did you expect to move from a group of two to groups of four or eight?

• As more people were added did it become more difficult to complete the activity? Why or why not?

Once students think about the activity, ask them to write about how this activity could link to writing a thesis in an essay. Then, open the room to discussion. Students should see many links, including thoughts like the following:

• When there are fewer components to a thesis, it is easier to understand. Too many ideas make it more difficult to follow, just like when it was harder for the entire group to stand but easier for a pair to do it.

• A thesis needs to be strong and able to stand on its own. If it falls apart, so does the paper.

- A successful thesis presents a clear path that can be built upon in the essay (the same way working with two people gave the pair a foundation upon which to work with three people and so on).

These ideas, however, do not entirely represent the construct of a thesis so it is a good idea to provide students with a handout that explains how you envision the idea of a thesis. (See "Two Models of Thesis Writing" on the following page.) Mention to students that these are just two ways to think about constructing a thesis and that a thesis involves moving parts, like the activity just completed. A thesis must have a specific topic and the angle in which the student plans to discuss that topic (like an overview of the essay); or what will be argued and how it will be done (like a map for the essay).

Assessment of Learning:

An excellent way to know if students learned about how to write a thesis is to ask them to practice it. Have students write three thesis statements that relate to a recently assigned paper and review them during the next class.

Alterations for Other Disciplines/Experiences:

In an alternate setting, this activity could be used to discuss group dynamics or teamwork. This activity could also be useful for art projects or for learning math equations or theories.

Two Models of Thesis Writing

- **THESIS AS AN OVERVIEW:**
  Specific Topic + Attitude/Angle/Argument = Thesis

  - Bad Example: *The North and South fought the Civil War for many reasons, some of which were the same and some different.*

    This thesis statement mentions a topic but has no angle or argument. It is far too general.

  - Good Example: *While both Northerners and Southerners believed they fought against tyranny and oppression, Northerners focused on the oppression of slaves while Southerners defended their own right to self-government.*

    This thesis statement mentions a subject (the Civil War) and a specific angle or interpretation on the War.

- **THESIS AS A MAP:**
  What you plan to argue/discuss + How you plan to argue it = Thesis

  - Bad Example: *Mark Twain's* Huckleberry Finn *is a great American novel.*

    While this sentence references what will be discussed, it in no way suggests how *Huckleberry Finn* is a great American novel.

  - Good Example: *Through its contrasting river and shore scenes, Twain's* Huckleberry Finn *suggests that to find the true expression of American democratic ideals, one must leave "civilized" society and go back to nature.*

    This sentence is complex and provides what the paper will discuss (*Huckleberry Finn*) and how it will discuss it (in terms of civility and nature).

Note: Example thesis statements from The Writing Center at the University of North Carolina at Chapel Hill's website

Lesson Plan 13 | Writing a Thesis, Lesson Two

Note: Thanks to Dr. Jim Hauser for providing this handout as part of his Writing Across the Curriculum Workshop at William Paterson University (slightly modified for the purposes of this text).

Materials:
- Copies of the handout provided at the end of this lesson plan
- Pens/pencils

Class Size:
Any

Required Time:
30 minutes

Location:
Classroom or other area where students can easily write on a hard surface

Objective:
- To practice crafting a thesis statement based on extracting information from texts

Student Preparation:
Come to class prepared with any notes or materials related to a topic for a recently assigned essay

Instructor Preparation:
Make copies of the handout included at the end of this lesson for each student.

Activity:
Explain to students that the two entries on the worksheet are from Napoleon's personal diary. Read each one aloud. Then, ask them to read the entries a second time silently to themselves and complete the questions at the bottom of the handout.

Discussion:

Request that a few students share their answers for the questions at the end of the worksheet. Then guide the discussion toward answering the following questions:

- How did you choose the four to six pieces of information?

- What from the text made those pieces seem more important than others?

- Did you base your summative statement on those four to six pieces of information? Or, how did those pieces of information assist you in shaping your summative statement?

- This summative statement is exactly like a thesis statement for an essay. It represents the core ideas that you developed after doing research (reading the excerpts), so how can we use this exercise in writing our own thesis statements?

The aim at the end of this exercise is that students see that what they did in this exercise—read for comprehension and important facts and make a statement based on that information—is exactly what they do when writing a paper for class. Some students will have taken different "angles" about Napoleon than others. This is okay; in fact, this is great! Show them that the same information can lead different people to different conclusions and all of them are correct, if they can be backed up with examples. This is why their opinions matter and how they form the central ideas of a paper and support those ideas with material from research.

Assessment of Learning:

Ask students to take out a recent assignment sheet that you have provided them as well as any notes or materials they have related to that assignment. Then, ask them to begin crafting their own thesis statement using the same steps they just completed with the in-class exercise: make a list of important extracted information and then craft a summative statement based off of that information. A few students could share thesis ideas with the class, with a partner (and get feedback), or you can walk around and help them one-on-one if the time is available to you.

You can ask them to take this even further by developing an entire outline for their paper. That step might be best performed a class session or two later, however, reviewing topic sentences and paragraphs before requiring an outline is recommended (see Lesson 14 in this book on those topics).

Alterations for Other Disciplines/Experiences:

While this handout provides diary entries from Napoleon, that material may not fit for your class (not that the entries here have to be entirely related to a course theme or recently assigned essay topic. In fact, there may be some benefit in practicing this thesis exercise on material unrelated to the course). You can alter the entries to fit whatever discipline your course or programming is working with. The only consideration, if altering the excerpts, is that they must provide enough information for students to generate a central idea.

Napoleon's Diary

Paris, January 1, 1798

> *Paris has a short memory. If I remain longer doing nothing, I am lost. In this great Babylon one reputation quickly succeeds another. After I have been seen three times at the theatre, I shall not be looked at again; I shall therefore not go very frequently.*

Saint Helena, March 3, 1817

> *In spite of all the libels, I have no fear whatever about my fame. Posterity will do me justice. The truth will be known: and the good I have done will be compared with the faults I have committed. I am not uneasy as to the results. Had I succeeded, I would have died with the reputation of the greatest man that ever existed. As it is, although I have failed, I shall be considered as an extraordinary man: my elevation was unparalleled, because unaccompanied by crime. I have fought fifty pitched battles, almost all of which I have won. I have framed and carried into effect a code of laws that will bear my name to the most distant posterity. I raised myself from nothing to be the most powerful monarch in the world. Europe was at my feet. I have always been of opinion that the sovereignty lay in the people. In fact, the imperial government was a kind of republic. Called to the head of it by the voice of the nation, my maxim was, la carriere est ouverte aux talens without distinction of birth or fortune, and this system of equality is the reason that your oligarchy hates me so much.*

*la carriere est ouverte aux talens = the career was open to talent

1. List four to six pieces of information extracted from the diary entries above.

2. Based on the information you've extracted, write down the most important summative statement you can about Napoleon.

Lesson Plan 14 | Paragraphs and Topic Sentences

NOTE: Jim Burke offers a similar lesson as well as additional options to expand on this lesson on pages 164-168 of his book *The English Teacher's Companion: A Complete Guide to Classroom, Curriculum, and the Profession, Third Edition.*

Materials:

Copies of a paragraph cut into strips with one sentence of the paragraph on each strip and one set of strips for each student (I like to keep them in envelopes so nothing gets lost). Alternatively, rearrange the sentences on a single piece of paper with lines next to each sentence for students to number in the correct order. This second option is less ideal since it is harder for students to read the paragraph in the correct order.

Class Size:

Unlimited

Required Time:

15-20 minutes

Location:

Classroom

Objective:

• To help students think about the organization and components of a paragraph in order to prepare them to write their own

No Student Preparation Needed

Instructor Preparation:

Find a paragraph that is well constructed and, possibly, connected to the course theme or current topic. Type that paragraph, separating the sentences onto their own lines in the document. Print as many copies as the number of students in the class (or groups you want them to work in) and then cut the separated sentences apart so each one is on its own strip of paper. Put one completed set (which is all of the sentences in the paragraph) into an envelope and repeat for the number of students (or groups) in the class. Print one copy of the paragraph in its correct, final form for yourself.

An example paragraph, for a college level writing course, taken from The Writing Center, University of North Carolina at Chapel Hill's website, could be:

> Slave spirituals often had hidden double meanings. On one level, spirituals referenced heaven, Jesus, and the soul, but on another level, the songs spoke about slave resistance. For example, according to Frederick Douglass, the song "O Canaan, Sweet Canaan" spoke of slaves' longing for heaven, but it also expressed their desire to escape to the North. Careful listeners heard this second meaning in the following lyrics: "I don't expect to stay / Much longer here. / Run to Jesus, shun the danger. / I don't expect to stay." When slaves sang this song, they could have been speaking of their departure from this life and their arrival in heaven; however, they also could have been describing their plans to leave the South and run, not to Jesus, but to the North. Slaves even used songs like "Steal Away to Jesus (at midnight)" to announce to other slaves the time and place of secret, forbidden meetings. What whites heard as merely spiritual songs, slaves discerned as detailed messages. The hidden meanings in spirituals allowed slaves to sing what they could not say.

Activity:

Give each student one envelope with the strips of paper inside or allow students to work in small groups with one envelope for each group. Tell the class that each strip has a sentence on it and that the goal is to put the sentences in order—matching the original construction of the paragraph. Allow five minutes to complete the task. Once time is up, ask a few students to read the sentences in the order in which they placed them—generally, there are many variations. Then on the board, write the proper order of a paragraph:

- Topic Sentence—informs the reader about the subject/idea of the paragraph and what it will cover

- 1st Main Point—backs up, furthers or explains the topic sentence

- 2nd Main Point—usually provides a reason for the 1st main point

- 3rd Main Point—either backs up the second main point or reinforces the topic sentence

- Conclusion/Transition—completes the topic and transitions into next paragraph

NOTE: Occasionally the main points may be more than one sentence, which is okay (and students should know that), but if so, include the entire main point on one strip of paper.

Ask the students to reconsider if their strips are in the correct order by evaluating if the order mirrors the requirements of the above criteria. Give them time to rearrange their sentences if they want. As some of them may have the correct order already, suggest that they think carefully and have reasons why they are making changes.

Discussion:

Move sentence-by-sentence through the paragraph to explain why each sentence is where it is. Here are some points to cover if using the example paragraph:

TOPIC SENTENCE: *Slave spirituals often had hidden double meanings.*

This sentence tells the readers that slave spirituals often had double meanings, which may or may not be true so further proof is needed.

FIRST MAIN POINT: *On one level, spirituals referenced heaven, Jesus, and the soul, but on another level, the songs spoke about slave resistance.*

Here is a sentence that declares two examples of what slave spirituals are about: spirituality as well as resistance. It provides support for the topic sentence, but not enough that the reader can take the author's word on it.

SECOND MAIN POINT: *For example, according to Frederick Douglass, the song "O Canaan, Sweet Canaan" spoke of slaves' longing for heaven, but it also expressed their desire to escape to the North. Careful listeners heard this second meaning in the following lyrics: "I don't expect to stay / Much longer here. / Run to Jesus, shun the danger. / I don't expect to stay." When slaves sang this song, they could have been speaking of their departure from this life and their arrival in heaven; however, they also could have been describing their plans to leave the South and run, not to Jesus, but to the North.*

Now, the author brings in an actual example of a song that has a double meaning—the specific double meaning referenced in the previous sentence. This is evidence that is starting to show the reader that the author is correct about her information and argument. But one example may not be convincing enough.

THIRD MAIN POINT: *Slaves even used songs like "Steal Away to Jesus (at midnight)" to announce to other slaves the time and place of secret, forbidden meetings.*

Here, the author provides a second example to support the claim that slave spirituals had double meaning. This sentence points to the earlier main points as well as the topic sentence.

CONCLUSION: *What whites heard as merely spiritual songs, slaves discerned as detailed messages. The hidden meanings in spirituals allowed slaves to sing what they could not say.*

This sentence sums up what the earlier sentences claimed. It also brings the paragraph to a natural end, a place where the reader feels like she has obtained enough information to agree or disagree with the author and that there is nothing more to add to the paragraph.

Assessment of Learning:

Students should write a paragraph on a topic of their choosing or on a topic you provide (something general like music or sports or their weekend or something connected to recent course material). Ask them to put a star next to the topic sentence, a one next to the first point, a two next to the second point, a three next to the third point, and to underline the first word of the conclusion sentence. Collect these papers to see if more explanation on the topic is needed in latter class periods. Alternatively, have a random selection of students explain their examples to the entire class to judge the effectiveness of the lesson.

Alterations for Other Disciplines/Experiences:

This activity could also be done to focus on topic sentences. Provide the student with the body of a paragraph and several possible topic sentences to address the body. Ask him to choose one and explain why the others do not work.

Additionally, this activity could illustrate how to put paragraphs together into a larger essay. Instead of moving sentence-by-sentence, however, the students would order a set of cut up paragraphs. At the beginning of the lesson, the instructor would explain the functions of the introduction, body paragraphs and conclusion in an essay instead of the function of each sentence in a paragraph.

With some adaptation, this activity could also be helpful in art class. Instead of broken up paragraphs, perhaps an art instructor could use something similar to teach how colors go together. A history class might be able to use this activity to assist in making timelines or understanding the order of certain historical events.

In an alternate setting, an activity similar to this could be used to teach skill sets, like the steps in lighting a stove. Alternatively, each student could write a thought or comment on a strip of paper about another student and put it in their envelope so everyone would have an envelope full of nice comments about themselves. These suggestions are clearly not the only applications of this activity. Think about how breaking something into pieces may assist a learning outcome that you have in mind—this activity may help with that.

Lesson Plan 15 | Using Transitions

Note: Adapted from *Lesson Plans for Teaching Writing* (Startt 15)

Materials:
A computer or pen/pencil and paper for each student

Class Size:
No more than 20, or a larger group broken up into groups of 15 to 20.

Required Time:
30 minutes

Location:
Classroom or computer lab

Objectives:
• To practice using transitions
• To understand how transitions function in writing

No Student Preparation Needed

Instructor Preparation:
Briefly discuss the purpose and function of transitions before this activity.

Activity:
Have each student sit in front of a computer or paper and pen. Provide a prompt from which students will begin writing. The prompt can be anything or specifically connected to course curriculum, but the example Startt provides in the original version of this exercise is "It was a dark and stormy night..." Allow ample time for the students to write, maybe five or so minutes.

Ask all the students to stand at the end of the time limit and turn on music of your choice (classical music is suggested as it soothes students and promotes thinking). While the music is playing students should walk from station to station and when the music stops, sit at the desk or computer where another student's work is laying. This is like musical chairs.

Wherever the last student left off, the current student should start writing with the next prompt. Startt suggests, "Out of nowhere appeared a..." The instructor should inform the students that it is important for the story to flow so they should consider how to transition into this, maybe abrupt, turn of events. Again, allow time to write.

Continue the "musical chairs" and provide another prompt for as many rounds as helpful and useful. Some ideas of other prompts could include:

- Suddenly,
- Back in the city,
- It was scary because
- Just then,
- From up above came a
- Nearby there was
- When it was over,
- But, later on,

Another option would be to have the students brainstorm a list of transitions that you provide in a specific order. Regardless, the last round should end in an "editing session" where each student revises the entire story in front of her. Remind the students to "keep it clean," otherwise, depending on your age group, you may get some inappropriate material that cannot be read aloud at the end of the activity.

An alternative way to run this exercise is to have the students sit in a circle and beginning writing with the initial prompt. Time them for about three minutes then ask them to pass their papers to the left. Repeat this until the original paper reaches the student who started it, who will then edit the story. You may have to increase the time limit for each pass as the students will need to read the entire story in order to maintain some level of coherence.

To make this more difficult, provide a few initial prompts, maybe six, and then stop providing them after that, forcing students to come up with their own transitions. They find this hard and sometimes the end products will turn into something full of tangents or unrelated material. It can make for good conversation once the activity is over as to why they didn't think of their own transitions once they were no longer provided.

An example of the end product of this activity from a class of college-level introductory writing students follows:

It was a dark and stormy night and I was gazing out the window looking at the puddles that were forming. Out of nowhere appeared a giant gorilla that ran through the streets grunting in a loud obscene manner. The grunting noise he was making kind of sounded like the theme song for "Family Guy." Just then the giant gorilla whipped out a banana costume and put it on while singing the "peanut butter jelly" song. It reminded me of one of my favorite episodes. I realized the gorilla was my friend. Nearby, there was a little gorilla who started to sing along with the giant gorilla. This was the first time I ever saw a gorilla sing so I sang along too. It was a big mistake because the gorillas did not like my voice. They started pounding their chests. So I started doing the same thing. I was happy they accepted me after this because I did not want to be eaten.

This example certainly takes some strange twists and turns and it is apparent where one student ended and another began. When my class discussed this example, we talked about where the transitions worked and did not work and how the inclusion of some information made the example harder to follow, like reference to Family Guy, which didn't seem to have a place in the rest of the paragraph. We connected this to trying to incorporate too many quotes into a paragraph or to choosing a piece of information from a text because it seemed good, but, in the end it makes the paragraph less cohesive than it could be otherwise. This is a common error made by students and showing how to avoid that mistake in a fun exercise like this helped them remember the concept later on in the semester. I would even write, "remove the Family Guy" on their drafts and they knew exactly what I meant and found the error on their own, which creates longer-lasting learning than if I had pointed it out myself.

You can use this example, if you would like, with your own students before or after they do the exercise themselves to help steer them away from making odd references just to be funny when you teach this lesson. While this lesson plan is geared toward showing students how transitions are important to writing, I shared the above discussion to also impart that this lesson can take you in other directions to talk about other significant writing-related issues.

Discussion:

Ask for volunteers to read stories aloud, allowing for as many to be shared as possible. Then open the discussion to transitions by asking questions like:

- Which of the stories shared today worked? Why?
- Which stories did not work as well? Why?
- How do transitions play a role in making these stories flow?
- Could you tell where one author ended and another began? How?
- Is flow important to more formal essays we write in this class? Why or why not?
- Do you care about how a piece of writing comes together when you are the reader? Have you ever stopped reading something because it did not flow?

Assessment of Learning:

One assessment of learning is to ask for a reflection paper on what new thoughts students have on transitions after the activity. Another assessment could be to ask students to take a current draft of a paper and circle all the places where transitions are used and star places where transitions are needed. This could be done with a student's own work or with a peers' work.

Alterations for Other Disciplines/Experiences:

This activity could be useful in multi-unit courses or programs to help students transition between activities. Instead of writing a story with the prompts laid out above, maybe the prompts could look like:

- The first activity we did was…
- Before it started I felt…
- Once it was over, I knew/felt/understood…
- Now we are doing…

If you are using this activity as a way to incorporate writing as a reflection tool for assistance in transition between activities or sections of a program, the instructor can decide if the writing is nonfiction or fiction, or even allow the students to choose.

Lesson Plan 16   Conclusions

Note: Adapted from *Silver Bullets* (Rhonke 130)

Materials:
- Advertisements from a magazine OR postcards (OR two exact replicas of a puzzle for each pair of students)
- Blank sheets of paper
- Pens/pencils

Class Size:
Unlimited

Required Time:
20-25 minutes

Location:
Classroom or outdoor space

Objectives:
- To help students understand the components required for a conclusion paragraph
- To illustrate that poor communication in a conclusion can skew the final message a reader takes away from an essay

No Student Preparation Needed

Instructor Preparation:
Prepare puzzle sets or images for students before class begins. If you choose to use advertisements/postcards, pick those that are not too complex or busy as students may find it difficult to replicate one that it complicated.

Activity:

Place students in pairs and ask them to sit back to back. Give one student in the pair an advertisement or a postcard and the other a sheet of white paper. This activity could also work by giving one student a completed, assembled puzzle, while the other student in the pair would have the exact same puzzle, but with pieces unassembled.

It is now the job of the student with the advertisement/postcard or the assembled puzzle to verbally communicate to his partner how to recreate (by drawing) or how to assemble the pieces in an order that will produce an exact copy of his pieces/advertisement. Students may complete this relatively quickly or it may take quite awhile depending on vocabulary and ability to work together. Once the pair has completed the task, the students can switch roles (pairs can switch images or puzzles with a different pair) and repeat.

Discussion:

Once each student has participated in both roles, bring the class back together. Begin by asking general questions:

- Were the recreated images a good replication of the original as far as size, shape, etc. (not drawing quality)? OR Did the puzzles match on the first try?

- What was easy or difficult about this activity?

- Was communication important to this activity? Why or why not?

- What words were useful? Did your partner ever use a word that you interpreted differently than he meant it?

After students think about the activity, ask them to free write about how they see this activity linking to writing a conclusion paragraph of an essay. Then, open the room to discussion. Students should see many links, including thoughts like the following:

- If you do not communicate clearly in the final paragraph of an essay, the reader might walk away with a set of ideas you did not intend, ultimately, seeing a different picture. This is problematic because then the paper did not effectively communicate all its points.

- Use the same vocabulary in the conclusion that you did in the essay so the reader will remember points you made earlier in your writing.

- A conclusion pulls together all the pieces of the essay, showing the completed "puzzle" or "picture."

- Think of the audience your essay is geared toward at the end of the paper and use wording that speaks to them.

These, of course, are not all the connections students may see between this activity and writing conclusions, but they are some major ones that should not be overlooked (so bring them up if the students do not). After completing this activity, review example conclusions with students or review the components of a conclusion that you would like to see in essays written for class.

Assessment of Learning:

There are two possible assessments that can be done after this activity. One is to ask students to write an actual conclusion, perhaps for a paper on which they are currently working. The second is to have students write a one-page reflection on how the activity helped them understand a conclusion in a new way.

Alterations for Other Disciplines/Experiences:

This activity could be adapted to address the conclusion of a course or the end of a phase of an experience.

Lesson Plan 17

Learning to Write a Research Paper

Note: Many thanks for Sam Steiger for help with this concept. Also, this lesson plan is very similar to an activity on the Wilderdom website, which should be noted here and could be reviewed for additional information ("Zoom").

Materials:
- *Zoom* by Istvan Banyai (2 copies, if you want to keep one as a reference)
- Pencils

Class Size:
20-30 people

Required Time:
60-80 minutes

Location:
Indoors or outdoors (a space that is large enough for students to move around)

Objectives:
- To illustrate how the multiple perspectives of numerous sources play a role in a research paper
- To demonstrate the various phases of writing and revising a research paper
- To develop critical thinking

No Student Preparation Needed

Instructor Preparation:
First, cut the binding off one copy of Zoom (keep the other copy whole as a reference). Consider laminating each page or putting them in protective sheet covers so they do not get damaged. Stick a blank label—that can be written on (in pencil)—of whatever size or color you choose to the back of each picture (if labels are colored, insure there is not a pattern that matches the order the pages go in the text). Then, mix up the pages of Zoom so they are not in order.

After reading through the activity directions, you may decide that it might be helpful to set up a line made of rope or masking tape to help guide students on where to place their pictures.

Activity:

In a large open space, free of obstacles, give each student one or two pages—depending on the class size—from the *Zoom* book. If a student has two pages try to make sure the pages are not from the same section of the book. Instead provide a student with a picture from the farm scene and the island scene, or the city and Arizona, and so on.

- Ask students to write their names in pencil on the label on the back of their sheets. They should not share their picture(s) with anyone else.

- Then, instruct students to take three to five minutes to examine their picture individually and think about how to describe that picture to someone else.

- After they have time to think about their pictures, explain that all the pictures are somehow related. Ask them to take the next 30-45 minutes (depending on the amount of class time available) to arrange the pictures in order. They cannot, at any time, show another person what their picture(s) looks like but can only verbally communicate what the picture looks like.

- When students think they have found where their particular picture goes in the story line, instruct them to place their picture on the ground with the blank side up (so the picture itself is turned toward the floor and cannot be seen) where they think it belongs. Inform the class members that after they put their individual pictures down, they may still need to describe it to others as the rest of the class continues to work and place their own pictures in the ordered pictures. Other students can call the person's name listed on the back of a page in order to get more description of the picture. However, no student except the one whose name is on the back of the picture may pick up or examine that page.

- When there are only eight or ten minutes left in the activity time period, tell the students that their time is running out and they should make their best guess as to where their picture fits and lay it down there. Once all the pages have been placed, have the students sit in a circle around the line of pictures so that each one of them can see. Start at one end and begin turning each one over to see which ones are in order and which ones are out of place.

Discussion:

Once all the photos are turned over, ask students to free write for four to six minutes about the activity, using all the time and writing even when they think they have nothing else to say. Use prompt questions like the following:

- While this activity seems to have nothing to do with writing or research, which is what this class is about, can you see any parallels or connections between this activity and the writing or research process?

- How does any part of this activity, from looking at the pictures, to communicating about them to others, to actually getting them in order relate to topics and ideas we've discussed in class about writing?

Asking students to write before they speak out loud helps them to think their thoughts through before communicating them (again, something that research asks them to do as well). Once they have written, ask them to share their thoughts. You want to guide the discussion so that students see why this activity is relevant to the course material. Ultimately, you want to help students see each page as the representation of one source they find during their research project and the activity, as a whole, as the representation of the writing and research process. Some connections that might be made follow:

TO THE RESEARCH PROCESS

- Students will often figure out how to do this activity by getting into small groups of people with like pictures and then figuring out how the pictures in the small groups go together before they figure out the larger picture. This can be related to sorting through research and grouping like sources together to make connections before being able to make connections between all sources.

- The pictures, when laid out correctly, are like a research question, guiding the reader to what the paper will cover.

TO THE WRITING PROCESS

- The pictures that are most zoomed out are like the introduction to a paper (general) while the most zoomed in ones are like a conclusion (specific). This also mimics an introduction, moving from the general to the specific (thesis). There are several interesting things students will see in how the visual product of this activity mimics the final structure of a research paper.

- Initially, many students will think about how the different sections (the farm, the city, Arizona) don't fit together, but through transition pictures, they all relate. This shows the importance of transitions in writing between paragraphs, between sentences, between major sections of a paper.

- In order to put the pictures in the right order, the language people used to describe the items is important. While some people will say there are Native Americans on the island pictures, for example, I've also heard student say: Blacks, Aboriginals, Indians, etc. Sometimes as a result of discordant language, students miss the connections. Here, the connection can be made that students need to use language in their papers that their audience will understand and they need to be consistent with that language throughout.

- Usually, by the end of the activity, one or two pictures are out of place. When this happens, discussion about how that confuses what the pictures are trying to do can come up. This can be related to putting ideas in the wrong order in the paper. A reader has to know the story starts with the globe to understand the city later on, just as a paper needs to set up a good foundation and create a framework within which it will work.

- Watch how the students react in the last few minutes of the exercise. Do they say "that's good enough!" and not double-check their work? Relate their actions to the revision process. This activity has a time-line, like most classroom-related papers (and eventually work in the professional realm). So, if they have an extra minute and don't use it, what does that say about the final product they have? Do they start rushing at the end and make mistakes? How would this impact a paper?

It is best if students come to these conclusions on their own (so that they mean more). Try to probe them with questions instead of providing answers. Try to not be too big a part of the conversation but instead let them talk to one another about what they learned from the activity. Starting with general questions often focuses their attention, then moving to more specific questions forces them to critically think about the activity. It is also helpful if you can bring up specific moments that occurred with those students. For example, if you noticed one student had a particularly hard time understanding another's descriptions, it can be a good idea to ask questions about communication directly to that pair. Another option is to generally state your observations about struggles (or successes) the class had and direct the questions to the entire class.

Consider the following questions:

1. What happened in this activity?

2. Did you find it easy or difficult?

3. Was it frustrating to try to communicate what your picture contained? Why or why not?

4. You now see where pictures were put in the correct order and where they were not. What do you think allowed for a successful placement and what caused misplacement?

5. Is it important to clearly communicate all your points in a paper like it was important to communicate aspects of your picture in this activity? Why or why not?

6. If each page represents an author that you find for your research paper, what connections can you make between this activity and writing your research paper?

7. How did you figure out which pictures (sources) were related and what did you do once you had a group of similar pictures?

8. How might this activity symbolize the entire writing process?

9. In writing classes, we often do peer review where someone else comments on your essays and gives you feedback to help you improve it. How does this activity help you see the role of peer review in writing and revising?

Assessments of Learning:

Ask students to write a one- or two-page response to the activity they just completed. Have them use free writing or double-entry journals to convey what they learned and the parallels they made.

Alterations for Other Disciplines/Experiences:

This activity could be used in art classes to show students how to pay attention to details like shapes, colors and so forth. It could also be used in language classes to help students use foreign words and practice vocabulary. In a program, it could be employed to discuss things like big picture versus small moments and other concepts that might help groups process the experience.

Lesson Plan 18 Referencing and Works Cited

Materials:
Pen/pencils and paper

Class Size:
Unlimited

Required Time:
15-20 minutes

Location:
Indoors or outdoors (a space that is large enough for students to move around)

Objectives:
- To allow student to think about when to reference another source in an essay
- To illustrate the importance of referencing information in its original context

Student Preparation:
Ask students to read your school's or organization's policy on academic integrity or honesty prior to arriving to class.

No Instructor Preparation Needed

Activity:
The idea behind this lesson plan is to play a game of telephone. Have the class sit in a circle and whisper a sentence to the first student who whispers it to the second and so on, until the sentence reaches the final student who says it out loud.

Play a second round where once the first sentence gets to the third person in the circle, a second sentence is started. A third round can be played with three sentences and so on.

Discussion:

Ask questions like the following:

- Why do you think the sentence did not remain the same from beginning to end?

- What could have been done to prevent the changes?

- In writing, is it important to accurately represent sources? Why or why not?

- Is quoting a source enough? What else has to be done?

- Is citing enough?

- Do we need to be careful about the context in which an author wrote and the way we write it into our pages? Why or why not?

- What does our policy on honesty and academic integrity say about all of this? How do you understand it better after this activity?

- Do you have any questions about that policy that you need clarified?

The idea is to connect alterations that happened to the sentence during the telephone game to problems with altering other sources in a research paper. The alterations come in many forms: not giving credit when it is due or misrepresenting an author's original work. Once you play telephone with the class, you can review on the board examples of how and when to cite as well as how to create a works cited page.

Assessment of Learning:

Give each student a contract to sign, something like an honor code (or even a copy of the school's or University's policy), that states that they will accurately represent other authors' work in their writing. Have them sign and return the contract to you along with a half-page reflection on what honesty and integrity in writing mean to them.

Alterations for Other Disciplines/Experiences:

In alternate settings, this activity might be helpful to discuss and illustrate ideas of communication, honesty, trust or accountability.

Lesson Plan 19 | Critiquing Papers and Giving Feedback: Your Own and Your Peers

Materials:
Various (see Instructor Preparation)

Class Size:
Various (see Instructor Preparation)

Required Time:
Various (see Instructor Preparation)

Location:
Instructor's choice

Objectives:
- To assist students in understanding the value of quality peer feedback
- To illustrate the importance of being critical but not harsh
- To help students approach their own writing with "fresh" eyes

No Student Preparation Needed

Instructor Preparation:
Choose any activity listed in this book and see the materials required, class size, required time, and location from that lesson. Some lessons in this book that might work best with this activity are Lesson 2, Lesson 4, Lesson 9 and Lesson 17. The activity can be long, short or part of another lesson you are teaching.

Activity:
Once the activity has begun, have two class members watch the rest of the class perform the activity and take notes on every action or behavior that was bad, negative or incorrect during the activity. Two other students should do the same but look for the positive actions and behaviors. When the activity is completed, ask those looking for the negative to stand up and give a report on their findings. After the negative report, have the class respond:

- How did the report make them feel?

- Did the negative feedback change their own ideas on how they performed?

- Did they agree with the report? Could they dismiss the findings if they didn't agree with it?

- Did it make them want to do the activity again?

Once the students answer those questions, ask those looking for the positive to give their report. Ask the students the same questions.

Then move the discussion toward peer review or revision of papers:

- How do you think it feels when someone only gets negative feedback on a paper? Do you think it makes them want to write more or is helpful to make them better?

- What about only positive comments? Does it move someone to the next level? Can you know how to improve with only that feedback?

- Should positive or negative comments come first? Does it matter?

- What are some rules we can follow as we review our own papers or the papers of our peers?

The discussion should assist the class in understanding how the feedback they provide in class and in peer review is important and helpful to other students, and they have a responsibility to do their job in the most constructive way possible. Then, discuss how peer review will work throughout the remainder of the course. Consider having the class, together, develop a list of group norms for peer review by which they will operate henceforth. (Integrating parts of Lesson 2 is a possibility here for establishing those norms.)

Alterations for Other Disciplines/Experiences:
In an experiential setting, this activity could assist with ideas of accountability and group dynamics.

Lesson Plan 20 | Developing a Story or Character (for Fiction)

Note: This lessons suggests using a wooded area as the location for the activity. Other options might be a nature museum, art galery, music room or playground.

Materials:
- Paper or notebooks
- Pens/pencils
- Clipboard or other

Class Size:
Any

Required Time:
30-45 minutes

Location:
Preferably a wooded area or an area with numerous natural objects

Objectives:
- To begin thinking about the important components of story (plot) development in creative writing
- To examine what makes a character round and believable

Student Preparation:
Students should read an excerpt on characterization from Janey Burroway's texts *Writing Fiction: A Guide to Narrative Craft, Eighth Edition* or *Imaginative Writing: The Elements of Craft, Third Edition*

Instructor Preparation:
Find an area where students can spread out but you will still be able to manage them safely and effectively. Focus this exercise on either story or character—decide what fits best into your curriculum.

Activity:

Ask students to put everything away but a writing utensil and paper (with something hard to write on—a notebook or binder). Either secure their belongings in the classroom or ask them to leave them in a central location near where they will be working. Walk them out to the location and describe the perimeters of the area within which they should work, this is so you can keep an eye on them to insure they are actually completing the work you assign and so no one gets separated from the class.

Then, when you tell them to, they will walk within the prescribed boundaries and find a natural object that appeals to them. It's best if you can have them do this before telling them what they will do with that object. If there are enough trees, ask each student to find a tree they like. If not, it can be any natural object. For twenty minutes, they are to personify that natural object and write its life story. The object should be given a gender, a childhood, an adulthood, and significant life events that made that object into the form and shape it is today. Suggest that they can make a bent tree a broken old man and write about how he became that way or perhaps that same tree is a child born disabled. Either way, they should feel the freedom to be creative. What they write should either A) convey the events that led the object to it's current state or B) describe those events from the object's perspective, thus fully developing the object's personality.

Decide if you want to ask them to be realistic or if they are allowed to incorporate science fiction or decide to leave those kinds of parameters out altogether. If possible, announce these instructions to the entire class at once or walk around to each student individually. If neither of these are possibilities, describe the activity before students separate and find their objects.

As they write, you may choose to float around the area where they are working or sit in a central location and let them work.

Discussion:

Refer to the first two chapters of this text for notes and considerations when students share creative, personal work, but it is your decision if you want to open the activity up to sharing or not, once it is completed. Alternatively, you can simply discuss components of either story development or character development further.

Assessment of Learning:

There are several options for assessment with this activity:

- Ask students to revise their work and turn in a polished version to you.

- Collect the assignment at the end of the class period.

- Do either of the above as well as collect a one to two page informal response on the importance of character or plot in creative writing.

Alterations for Other Disciplines/Experiences:

This activity could easily be adapted to alternative settings to allow students to explore nature, explore ideas about a recent program or event or simply write about something unrelated to recent experiences and course material. Any form of writing is the practice of writing and sometimes a break from "formal" curriculum to do something creative can be useful.

This activity could also be useful in drawing or visual art classes to explore different perceptions, stories and points of view on particular objects through visual mediums.

Lesson Plan 21 | Working With Language (for Poetry)

Note: Many thanks to Lauren Grodstein of Rutgers University-Camden for helping with this concept.

Materials:
- Pens/pencils and paper
- Chalkboard, whiteboard or other means of display

Class Size:
Any

Required Time:
30-45 minutes

Location:
Classroom or other area where students can easily write on a hard surface

Objectives:
- To utilize form poetry as a means of introduction to the genre
- To demonstrate the importance of word choice in poetry

No Student Preparation Needed

Instructor Preparation:
The sestina is the form of poetry that I use to teach this lesson (other forms can work as well with some adjustments). Begin with a basic understanding of a sestina, which is a poem comprised of six lines in each of six stanzas. The poem form is highly structured as the same set of six words end a line of each stanza, but in a different order each time. Once the first stanza is written, the ending words are each given a corresponding number in the order 123456. In the second stanza, those same words end each line in the order 615243, in the third 364125, then 532614, then 451362 and finally 246531. A seventh stanza, a tercet, generally accompanies the above six stanzas with the first line containing words 6 and 2, the second line 1

and 4 and the last 5 and 3. However, other versions exist with a couplet at the end. Many times poets play with the words. For example, if "tree" was one word, "trees" would also be acceptable. Another example, in Scott Oliver's Sestina on page 123, "throughout" has also been used as "threw out."

Following the activity and discussion, you could show the class a published sestina and look at how it works—two are included at the end of this lesson. Ashberry's sestina has a topic that students new to poetry might find accessible and funny: Popeye, but which might not be appropriate for younger audiences due to the final tercet. Thus, Oliver's sestina might be better and slightly more traditional. Of course, there are many great sestinas including ones written by Ezra Pound, Elizabeth Bishop, and Marilyn Hacker. Find one that suits your needs and class material and understand how it works so you can discuss it in class.

> **Note:** A sestina may be too complicated a form of poetry for young students. Consider using an alternate form with younger groups if you think it would be helpful. See the "Alterations" section at the end of this lesson for more information.

Activity:

Ask the students for six words. You can choose to tell them they will be writing a poem with them or not. You may want to encourage them to pick a variety of words: colors, verbs, nouns or just see what comes up. If a really difficult word is chosen, you might ask them to change it. Then write those six words on the board and number them. Then provide them with the structure of the sestina. Explain how each stanza words and how the words should be ordered (see Instructor Preparation). Then ask them to write their own sestina using those words.

Discussion:

Writing a sestina can take quite awhile so students may not be able to complete all six stanzas and the tercet in the thirty minutes you provide. However, give them as much time as you can afford and then ask a few students if they would be willing to share their creations. If you have a small group, everyone can share or pass if they so desire. Then, if this activity is used at the beginning of a poetry unit, you can guide the discussion toward a conversation on craft asking questions like:

- What was difficult about writing a sestina?

- What was easy about it?

- Was it nice to have a structure to work with or confining?

- What do you think about the words we worked with? What would you change about them? Would you have picked something different if you knew what we were doing with them?

- What can we learn from this exercise about poetry?

- What effect does the repetition of words have on the reader?

- What about some of the sestinas your classmates shared seemed effective and why do you think so?

Discussions Specific to the Poems Included in This Lesson:

When Discussing Ashberry's poem it's important to note that some of the characters may be unfamiliar to students, like Sea Hag and Wimpy. This is because Ashberry focused on the newspaper comic for his poem, not the cartoon. You might ask students to think about how the title (pastoral and agrarian) relates to the poem as whole. Ashberry is known for his ironic titles that may suggest the poem is about one thing when really it is about another. In Ashberry's sestina there is no reference to rutabagas or farming or the agrarian world in general (although this is, historically, the topic of many sestinas); so, what effect does that disconnect have on the reader? Ask students to think about the sestina as a puzzle or a code. How do the pieces fit together? How can it be decoded? This may help them approach Ashberry's poem.

When discussing Oliver's poem, notice that this sestina places attention to the importance of end words and their effect on the narrative. First, three of the end words (cup, throughout, and still) are able to be used more openly (for example, "throughout" and "threw out" and "through, out") which allows the author to free up the narrative and gives the reader something that is not so repetitious. Asking students what words they think might be "easier" to use in a sestina is a good way of introducing this form. The other words (dove, tree, and blue) are more essential to the narrative in the poem. Again, asking the students to substitute like words in their own work can remind them that there is wiggle room in all writing. Oliver's sestina provides a simple enough story that does not jar a reader in an already jarring form. He employs clear symbols for "good" and "bad," which allow a reader to focus on what is being suggested, and not merely what is written. Ask the students how they think the author feels about war, or even the form itself, this is a good way of having the students discuss the connection technique and style have with topic and meaning. This sestina could be part of a class discussion about what freedoms writers have in even the strictest of forms.

Assessment of Learning:

To assess learning from this exercise, ask students to complete the sestina for homework or assign the form as part of a poetry packet they may complete for the entire unit. You can decide if you want students to continue to work with the same words that were provided in class or if you'll allow them to develop new words for the assignment.

Another assessment would be to have the students analyze the sestina you shared with them or one they find on their own. They could write a brief response paper or come into class prepared to give a short presentation. This would certainly show if they understood how to deduct meaning from within a poem and if they can consider how form works within poetry.

Alterations for Other Disciplines/Experiences:

This exercise could also work for a lesson on the importance of word choice or on how to create images, either for poetry, fiction or nonfiction. This activity could be done with a poem of any form, really. The sestina is a particularly challenging form, so you can swap in a sonnet or other form if it better suits your class' needs. Finally, another alteration for this lesson plan is to focus on the revision of a poem instead of the crafting of it.

Farm Implements and Rutabagas in a Landscape

by John Ashberry (Ashberry xx)

The first of the undecoded messages read: "Popeye sits
  in thunder,
Unthought of. From that shoebox of an apartment,
From livid curtain's hue, a tangram emerges: a country."
Meanwhile the Sea Hag was relaxing on a green couch: "How
  pleasant
To spend one's vacation en la casa de Popeye," she
  scratched
Her cleft chin's solitary hair. She remembered spinach

And was going to ask Wimpy if he had bought any spinach.
"M'love," he intercepted, "the plains are decked out
  in thunder
Today, and it shall be as you wish." He scratched
The part of his head under his hat. The apartment
Seemed to grow smaller. "But what if no pleasant
Inspiration plunge us now to the stars? For this is my
  country."

Suddenly they remembered how it was cheaper in the country.
Wimpy was thoughtfully cutting open a number 2 can of spinach
When the door opened and Swee'pea crept in. "How pleasant!"
But Swee'pea looked morose. A note was pinned to his bib.
  "Thunder
And tears are unavailing," it read. "Henceforth shall
  Popeye's apartment
Be but remembered space, toxic or salubrious, whole or
  scratched."

Olive came hurtling through the window; its geraniums scratched
Her long thigh. "I have news!" she gasped. "Popeye, forced as
  you know to flee the country
One musty gusty evening, by the schemes of his wizened,
  duplicate father, jealous of the apartment
And all that it contains, myself and spinach
In particular, heaves bolts of loving thunder
At his own astonished becoming, rupturing the pleasant

Arpeggio of our years. No more shall pleasant
Rays of the sun refresh your sense of growing old, nor the
   scratched
Tree-trunks and mossy foliage, only immaculate darkness and
   thunder."
She grabbed Swee'pea. "I'm taking the brat to the country."
"But you can't do that--he hasn't even finished his spinach,"
Urged the Sea Hag, looking fearfully around at the apartment.

But Olive was already out of earshot. Now the apartment
Succumbed to a strange new hush. "Actually it's quite pleasant
Here," thought the Sea Hag. "If this is all we need fear from
   spinach
Then I don't mind so much. Perhaps we could invite Alice the Goon
   over"--she scratched
One dug pensively--"but Wimpy is such a country
Bumpkin, always burping like that." Minute at first, the thunder

Soon filled the apartment. It was domestic thunder,
The color of spinach. Popeye chuckled and scratched
His balls: it sure was pleasant to spend a day in the country

Doves' Blue Cups Throughout Still Trees

by Scott Oliver (Oliver 23-24)

War needs another poem. Even the doves
are marching single file into the blue
with chests pluming abroad in order to cup
the scent of sun and son's blood spilled
throughout
young fields. They move on while everything
is still
because there is no use going back to the
tree.

Can any re-ascend the leaves of nesting trees?
Can there ever be but two loveasily doves?
If the wind's pact is that it'll never be still,
why even arch our wings into the wide blue
back to mothers, mothers who threw out
weakwings with only our beggar's cup?

Some do anything in order to fill that cup,
sharpen men-tall spears—hundreds—from
fallen trees,
kisswarm sap running with that day's sun
throughout
it. And hawks nest in the sky like old snipers.
Doves
with neatly pressed feathers inspect a violent
blue
sky, keeping an eye on the one they love. Still,

they know that lovebirds are the myths of
peace. Still,
each dove would forget this war and empty
each cup
to the sky, asking of it nothing, but why so
blue?
before thatching a hundred spears to make
one tree
that in years of war, won't house all the doves
but might fit a squad of battlangst hawks
throughout.

When the war is worn to the nub and
through, out
roll talliers like tanks—like eggs. They're
counting still.
Lain along the young field, two by two, the
doves
grasp what's left of never filled, or emptied,
cups.
Beak and breast plume like tombstones or
fallen trees.
A few lone hawks screech between the sky's
silent blue

that never knew until that second that it was
blue.
What shouldn't be mourned or forgotten of
wars throughout
and above the trees, and who'll plant a new
tree
when each leaf and half of the doves fall and
keep still?
Will the hawks, who have the world of time
now, cup
their wings and hold the rotten smoke of
marching doves?

Watching trees turn blue,
mourning the lone doves throughout,
so still lay the cups.

Lesson Plan 22
Choosing a Story and Integrating Research (for Creative Nonfiction)

Materials:
Pens/pencils and paper

Class Size:
Any

Required Time:
30-45 minutes

Location:
Classroom or other area where students can easily write on a hard surface

Objective:
- To consider the entirety of a personal story instead of a single viewpoint

Student Preparation:
Come to class with a list of life events or experiences to write about. If possible, they could also choose one event they want to write about before class and interview anyone they can who was involved in that event: parents, grandparents, friends, etcetera.

No Instructor Preparation Needed

Activity:
From the list the students' have prepared, ask them to choose one event about which they would like to write. Ask them to list all the characters (people) involved in the event. Then on a separate sheet of paper, they should write the story from each of those person's point-of-view. If they have already interviewed all these people, it will be much easier. This could be in a bulleted form, in complete sentences, or however you would like them to do it. You can also have them share this with a partner or the class as a whole.

Discussion:

Once they have finished, ask them questions like the following:

- What did you learn from looking at an event from multiple perspectives? Did your opinion change about the event after doing this?

- Were some perspectives more important than others? Which ones and why?

- If you were to write this story, completely, which of these perspectives would be important to consider and why?

- Since this would be your story, how would you incorporate these other perspectives in a way that would not confuse the reader?

- How might your own memory be skewed about this event? Would it be worth interviewing someone else to get more information and, thus, write a more well-informed essay?

The aim here is to help students approach writing about a personal experience in a more well-rounded manner than they might if they only considered their own perspective on the events. This brings in the element of research and interviewing and you can take the discussion there. Remind them that just because they experienced something does not mean that anyone else wants to read about it. In fact, most people do not care about what happens in the lives of anyone other than their loved ones. In order for a stranger to read a student's essay, tell them that the stranger has to find something about it interesting or identifiable. This is where research can help to contextualize events in a more universal manner.

Assessment of Learning:

Ask students to complete this essay for a graded assignment. Alternatively, have them write an informal response about what they learned about creative nonfiction from this lesson.

Alterations for Other Disciplines/Experiences:

This exercise could work for fiction as well. Have students write the plot of a story from the perspective of each character involved. Alternatively, they could choose the profession of their main character and come to class prepared with research on that profession, using it as they craft that character.

Lesson Plan 23 | Crafting a Lede (for Journalism)

Note 1: Much of the information for this lesson plan came from Robert M. Knight's book *The Craft of Clarity: A Journalistic Approach to Writing*

Note 2: Lesson Plan 10: Working on Clarity can be used in conjunction with this lesson to focus on headline writing instead of lede writing.

Materials:
- Pens/pencils and paper
- Chalkboard, Whiteboard or other means of display

Class Size:
Any

Required Time:
30-45 minutes

Location:
Classroom or other area where students can easily write on a hard surface

Objectives:
- To work with the lede, or opening of a journalistic article
- To demonstrate the necessity for clarity

Student Preparation:
Bring in a newspaper article or two regarding recent events.

Instructor Preparation:
Find one current event to read to students at the beginning of this exercise.

Activity:
Read the newspaper article you brought aloud to the class (you might need to read it twice). Students should be taking notes on important details and other

information as you read. Ask them to describe to you the important components of journalistic writing. The list will vary but should include the following:

- Clarity
- Attention-grabbing
- Interesting/Captivating
- Current
- Well-written, specific, concise (big vocabulary is not always good writing, especially in journalism)
- Logical
- Represents events in order
- Unbiased
- Backed up by facts or research
- Knows the audience and is written to it

With that in mind they should develop three options for the opening sentence of the article you just read aloud to them. A lede can extend beyond the first sentence and be considered the "opening" of the article, so if that better suits your needs, they can do that instead or in addition to writing three first sentences. Remind them that most common newspapers lead with summary ledes that contain Who, What, Where and When. The Why contains details and specifics that are addressed in the latter parts of the article. Lede's can also be anecdotal or creative. Students could try to write one of each for this exercise. You can also put the following examples up on the board for them to refer to:

- SUMMARY LEDE: "A 15-year-old boy died early Wednesday after being critically wounded in a gang-related shooting on the West Side" (Knight 33).
- CREATIVE LEDE: "The mayor of one of China's most exotic cities today visited the fertile flatlands of northwest Ohio to sample some products of a Chinese-American food factory. He pronounced the fare good— for American tastes" (Knight 35).
- ANCEDOTAL LEDE: "The phone rang at Robert Walker's suburban Denver home on Saturday in October. At the other end of the line was John White, the company's South Carolina Broker" (Knight 36).

Review each of the above (or find examples from a recent paper) and mention how they each still cover the first 4Ws but in different ways. Point out how none begin with quotations or questions, but are informative and attention-grabbing instead.

Discussion:

Ask students to share their attempts at ledes with the class. Have a few students write their ledes on the board, then push the class to figure out how to make them better. Point to the concepts of active voice, being concise and informative and being interesting.

Assessment of Learning:

Have the students take the newspaper articles they brought to class and partner with another student. The first student should choose one article (or both if there is time) and give his partner only the important information she needs to know about the event. She should take notes while he speaks. The she should do the same for him. Then each student should write the lede for that article. Once both are done, the students can see the original articles and compare their ledes to the published version. As the instructor, collect this along with the article to see how the students did.

Alterations for Other Disciplines/Experiences:

This exercise could be useful for teaching topic sentences. However, since topic sentences don't always include information like the 4Ws, that would need to be made clear and the focus would be on clarity instead. Also, this activity could be great for teaching students how to use active voice.

Lesson Plan 24 Finding Voice

Materials:
- Paper
- Pen/pencils

Class Size:
Any

Required Time:
30-35 minutes

Location:
Classroom or other area where students can easily write on a hard surface

Objectives:
- To demonstrate the use of voice in writing
- To illustrate the various voices that exist in one story
- To convey how different perspectives can alter both what is read and what is written

Student Preparation:
Have students come to class with an article from the newspaper that involves three or more distinct people.

No Instructor Preparation Needed

Activity:
Begin by discussing the concept of voice in writing. In his book *Coming to Terms with Experience Through Writing*, Scott Oury talks about voice as "central to writing" (8). He encourages readers to think of voice as someone speaking and to notice the features of voice, which he says are:

- Tone
- Pitch: high or low
- Intensity: loud or soft
- Pace: fast or slow, smooth or choppy
- Rhythm and accent
- The use of words and phrases that come with a particular tone: so? so what, get real, oh, face it, you don't say, really, really?
- The use of words that mimic particular sense impressions: slap, murmur, tickle, bubble, slice, crash, soft, tiny, gigantic, awesome (Oury 8).

Remind students that generalizations are not part of voice. Ask them to think about friends and family and how they speak or act. Do they all have the same inflection in their voice? If they were to mimic their mother and their father would it sound the same? Their sister and their best friend? Remind them to think about these intricacies when going into the activity.

In small groups, have the students recount the current event they brought in to the other group members. They should take no more than two minutes each to do this. Then, the group can choose one event to work with, or if you'd prefer to have them work individually, they can. Ask them to develop a list of people involved in the event.

Once they have done that, the student should write a statement to the press (or another entity that you determine) about the event from the point of view of three (if there are more, they should choose three) of the people. Before writing the statement, they should create a list of the characteristics of each person based upon what is said in the article. Provide them with some questions to ask:

- How old is this person?
- What is the gender of this person?
- Where is this person from?
- If quoted in the article, how does this person speak? What can I learn about this person because of that?
- Is this person described physically in any way?
- How was this person involved in this event and how does it help me understand them?

As they work, move from group to group and see how they are doing or if they need help. Consider giving them a time limit or a length limit as they write if time is an important consideration.

Discussion:

Ask for the groups to read their statements aloud to the class and then invite discussion. Some questions you might explore could be:

- Why did you write that person's statement that way?

- What contributed to how you wrote it?

- Could other groups tell the difference between the three people? Why or why not?

Assessment of Learning:

There are several ways to assess learning in this activity. The first would be to collect the in-class work and review. The second would be to ask for a free write from the students on the activity. Alternatively, a reading can be assigned and students can repeat this exercise independently at home for homework. Another fun assessment would be to allow them to write a piece of fiction or make a cartoon strip using three distinct voices.

Alterations for Other Disciplines/Experiences:

This activity would be incredibly useful in the creative writing classroom. It might also be helpful to a class using public speaking. Another option would be to ask students to use this activity to consider audience instead of or in addition to voice. If you want to focus on audience ask students to choose one person (or character) in the current event and have that person talk to other actors/characters in the story. For example, discussion would focus around how a character speaks differently to her older neighbor than a young child. Students can also write a statement from that character to the press, which then also brings in the element of point-of-view. Point-of-view can be used for literary interpretation and creative writing classes, but also, in an alterative educational setting, to offer insights into the fact that within every experience there are many viewpoints.

Works Cited

Ashberry, John. "On Farm Implements and Rutabagas in a Landscape." Poets.org. Academy of American Poets. 2011. Web. 19 Aug. 2011.

Bean, John C. *Engaging Ideas: The Professor's Guide to Integrating Writing, Critical Thinking, and Active Learning in the Classroom.* San Francisco, CA: Jossey-Bass, 2001. Print.

Beidler, Peter. "A Turn Down the Harbor." *Journal of Experiential Education.* 3.2 (1980): 24-32. Print.

---. "English in the Treetops." *Journal of Experiential Education.* 8.3 (1985): 34-41. Print.

Bennett, Samantha. *That Workshop Book: New Systems and Structure for Classrooms That Read, Write and Think.* Portsmouth, NH: Heinemann, 2007. Print.

Berthoff, Ann E. *The Making of Meaning: Metaphors, Models and Maxims for Writing Teachers.* Upper Montclair, NJ: Boynton/Cook Publishers, Inc., 1981. Print.

Brew, Alan. "Writing Activities: A Primer for Outdoor Educators." ERIC Clearinghouse on Rural Education and Small Schools. (2003): 1-6. Print.

Burke, Jim. T*he English Teacher's Companion: A Complete Guide to the Classroom, Curriculum, and the Profession, Third Edition.* Portsmouth, NH: Heinemann, 2008. Print.

Bynum Pickle, Melody R. *Writing's Place in Outdoor Experiential Education: A Study of How Outdoor Educators Use and Value Writing in Experiential Education Settings.* Diss. Indiana University of Pennsylvania, 2007. Ann Arbor: UMI, 200., Print.

Crosby, April. "A Critical Look: The Philosophical Foundations of Experiential Education." *The Theory of Experiential Education: A Collection of Articles Addressing the Historical, Philosophical, Social and Psychological Foundations of Experiential Education.* Eds. Karen Warren, Mitchell Sakofs and Jasper S. Hunt, Jr. Dubuque, IA: Kendal/Hunt Publishing Company. 3-13. Print.

Dewey, John. *Experience and Education.* New York, NY: Macmillan Publishing Company, 1938. Print.

Elbow, Peter. *Writing Without Teachers, Second Edition.* New York, NY: Oxford University Press, 1998. Print.

Evans, Nancy J, Deanna S. Forney and Florence Guido-DiBrito. *Student Development in College: Theory, Research and Practice.* San Francisco, CA: Jossey-Bass, 1998. Print.

Frank, Laurie. *Journey Toward the Caring Classroom: Using Adventure to Create Community.* Oklahoma City, OK: Woods 'N' Barnes Publishing, 2004. Print.

Hauser, Jim and Sharon Hanks. *Writing Across the Curriculum Workshop.* William Paterson University. Atrium, Wayne, NJ. 13 Jan. 2009. Lecture.

Hunt Jr., Jasper S. "Dewey's Philosophical Method and Its Influence on His Philosophy of Education." *The Theory of Experiential Education.* Eds. Karen Warren, Mitchell Sakofs and Jasper S. Hunt Jr. Boulder, CO: Kendall/Hunt Publishing. 23-32. Print.

---. "Philosophy of Adventure Education." *Adventure Programming.* Eds. John C. Miles and Simon Priest. State College, PA: Venture Publishing, Inc, 1991. 115-122. Print.

Knight, Robert M. *The Craft of Clarity: A Journalistic Approach to Writing. 2nd ed.* Ames: Iowa State Press, 2003. Print.

Lakoff, George and Mark Johnson. *Metaphors We Live By.* Chicago, IL: The University of Chicago Press, 1980. Print.

Merriam-Webster Online Dictionary. Merriam-Webster Incorporated. 2011. Web. 1 April 2011.

Oliver, Scott. "Doves' Blue Cups Throughout Still Trees" *Slush: Rutgers University-Camden Graduate Creative Writing Anthology.* Camden: Rutgers University-Camden, 2011. 23-24. Print.

Oury, Scott. *Coming to Terms with Experience Through Writing.* Santa Fe, NM: CreateSpace, 2007. Print.

Priest, Simon. "The Semantics of Adventure Programming." *Adventure Programming.* Eds. John C. Miles and Simon Priest. State College, PA: Venture Publishing, Inc, 1991. 111-114. Print.

Project Adventure. Project Adventure. N.d. Web. 1 April 2011.

Rapparlie, Leslie. "How Do We Learn? An Exploration into John Dewey's Pattern of Inquiry." *Teaching Adventure Education: Theory and Best Practices.* Eds. Bob Stremba and Christian Bisson. Champaign, IL: Human Kinetics, 2009. 128-134. Print.

Rhonke, Karl E. *Silver Bullets: A Guide to Initiative Problems, Adventure Games and Trust Activities.* Dubuque, IA: Kendall/Hunt Publishing Company, 1984. Print.

Stanchfield, Jennifer. *Tips & Tools: The Art of Experiential Group Facilitation.* Oklahoma City, OK: Woods 'N' Barnes Publishing, 2007. Print.

Startt, Bonnie. "Lesson 8—Musical Chairs: Practicing Transitions." *Lesson Plans for Teaching Writing.* Ed. Chris Jennings Dixon. Urbana, IL: National Council of Teachers of English. 15-16. Print.

Tovani, Cris. *Do I Really Have to Teach Reading? Content Comprehension, Grades 6-12.* Portland, ME: Stenhouse Publishers, 2004. Print.

"What is Service Learning?" *National Service-Learning Clearinghouse.* ETR Associates. 2011. Web. 1 April 2011.

The Writing Center, University of North Carolina at Chapel Hill. University of North Carolina at Chapel Hill, 2007. Web. 30 June 2010.

Wurdinger, Scott D. *Using Experiential Learning in the Classroom: Practical Ideas for All Educators.* Lanham, MD: Scarecrow Education, 2005. Print.

Young, Art. *Teaching Writing Across the Curriculum, Third Edition.* Upper Saddle River, NJ: Prentice Hall Resources for Writing, 1999. Print.

"Zoom." Wilderdom.com. Wilderdom. 12 July 2009. Web. 28 July 2011.

Works Consulted

Banyai, Istvan. *Zoom*. New York, NY: Viking, 1995. Print.

Burroway, Janet. *Imagintive Writing: The Elements of Craft, Third Edition*. New York, NY: Longman, 2010. Print.

Burroway, Janet, Elizabeth Stuckey-French and Ned Stuckey-French. *Writing Fiction: A Guide to Narrative Craft, Eight Edition*. New York, NY: Longman, 2011. Print.

Haven, Cynthia. "The New Literacy: Stanford Study Finds Richness and Complexity in Students' Writing." *Stanford Report*. 12 October 2009. Web. 20 Junly 2011.

King, Stephen. *On Writing: A Memoir of the Craft*. New York, NY: Pocket Books, 2000. Print.

Lansing, Alfred. *Endurance: Shackleton's Incredible Voyage*. New York, NY: McGraw-Hill, 1959. Print.

Miller, Lisa C. *Make Me a Story: Teaching Writing Through Digital Storytelling*. Portland, ME: Stenhouse Publishers, 2010. Print.

Morrell, Margot and Stephanie Capparell. *Shackelton's Way: Leadership Lessons from the Great Antarctic Explorer*. New York, NY: Viking, 2001. Print.

Rilke, Rainer Maria. *Letters to a Young Poet*. Cambridge, MA: Harvard University Press, 2011. Print.

Shackleton: The Greatest Survival Story of All Time. Dir. Charles Sturridge. A&E Home Video, 2002. DVD.

Wurdinger, Scott D. and Julie A. Carlson. *Teaching for Experiential Learning: Five Approaches that Work*. Lanham, MD: Rowman & Littlefield Education, 2010. Print.

Index

About the Author

Leslie Rapparlie has been a part of the education and writing fields since 2001. She began as an adventure trip guide, then directed a collegiate outdoor education program. In 2007, she started instructing creative writing and composition at Rutgers University-New Brunswick.

Photo by Christine Merson

Leslie received her Bachelor of Arts in Creative Writing and Environmental Studies from Gettysburg College, a Master of Science in Experiential Education from Minnesota State University, Mankato and a Master of Fine Arts in Fiction from Rutgers University-Camden.

Her short stories have appeared in *South Philly Fiction* and *The Broken Plate* and she contributed an article to *Teaching Adventure Education: Best Practices*. Leslie has also co-authored four other texts from the Creative Company on adventure sports.

Born in Ohio, she has called many places home, including Colorado, Pennsylvania, Minnesota, Virginia and New Zealand. In her spare time she practices and teaches yoga, spends time outside, skis, rock climbs and travels. She currently teaches at Montclair State University in New Jersey.

www.leslierapparlie.com

Notes

Notes